1

At Long Last

A STORY OF LOVE + HOPE

Erin Morris

Princess Publishing

Princess Publishing

At Long Last
Copyright © 2015 Erin Morris

ISBN   978-0-692-56038-9

All Scripture quotations, unless otherwise indicated, are taken from the Holy Bible, *New International Version.*

Cover design: Erin Morris
Cover photography: Daniel Morris
Editor: Candy Girdlestone
Interior Design: Erin Morris

Printed in the United States of America

For those who feel forgotten.

Contents

Introduction: At Long Last
Author's Note

Part One
1,710 MILES AND 27 YEARS APART

Part Two
I'LL BE WAITING

Part Three

COWBOY AND ME: A LOVE STORY

Introduction: At Long Last

This book is not simply a fairytale or "just" a love story. It is two separate stories – each with its own characters, joys, heartaches, and lessons. By God's hand and grace, these two stories have artfully melded into *one*.

At Long Last: A Story of Love and Hope is a testimony of God's plan in two individual lives; an example of His unfailing grace, merciful goodness, and specific care. It's a picture of how the Lord weaves beautiful things out of brokenness. Like the backside of a quilt in the midst of being sewn: messy, disorganized, and full of random threads. But the front side? A beautiful work of craftsmanship, every stitch purposeful and planned.

Writing an account of your love story is fairly easy. It's all bliss! Perfect pictures of smiles, bubbly laughter, kisses, and pink sunsets. Sweet anecdotes and stories that make reader's hearts go pitter-patter. So romantic, happy, and magazine-worthy.

But writing the things that happened *before* the sparkling wedding day full of white lace and wide smiles: the not so fairytale-like moments, the heartache, the pain, the confusion, the messiness, the humiliation (at times), the pity, the fear, the loneliness, and doubt? Not so easy. Our love story did not come effortlessly or quickly, flawlessly or magically. It was no movie script. It was real life.

This story I am about to tell you is full of miracles. God dipped down into the lives of two imperfect people and chose to do something truly special and extravagantly kind.

As a blogger, I write many things on my little space on the Internet, my home that you can visit at: www.itserinmorris.com. I began my blog almost four years ago as a place I shared my heart. Single and praying for my future husband at the time, I passionately wrote about waiting. I encouraged women to trust the Lord with their love stories: to pray for their future husbands, to focus on their relationship with God, to live differently than the culture around them, and to believe with hopeful hearts for a beautiful romance. A romance that shines so the whole wide world can see how great Jesus is and how He weaves redemption and grace into our mess and has the power to make our wildest dreams come true.

So, I put myself out there and wrote very honestly about how I chose to wait for "my man," to save sex for marriage, and to pray for my future husband. It is not everyone's story or heart, but it was mine. I loved my God and my future husband, fiercely. And I chose not to settle for anything less than God's best for me. I prayed for a man of integrity and honor, who would treat me like a princess and treasure me as gold. It was a bold, fearless stand. I met with some criticism, but mostly encouragement. In my community, I knew just a handful of young women and men who took the same vows. Through my blog, I found there were even more across the world!

I knew, with every fiber in my soul, that the God who hung the moon and named each star in the night sky cared deeply for me and had a wonderful plan for my life. If God created me and crafted a plan for my life, why would He not write the story of my love life? Little did this California girl know that way out in Oklahoma there was a young man praying for his future wife, making the same vows, and dreaming of the same things.

Along the way, our two dreaming souls faced discouragement, loss, and confusion at seemingly unanswered prayers, and disillusionment with the harsh realities of this crazy world we live in. Our bold stances to "wait" and pray for our future spouses were fiery at first, and then at times they lagged. In days of gloom, shadow, and sorrow, there were times we could hardly see or even remember the dreams. But light broke through, as it does, and hearts were mended and dreams came true, as they should. Prayers were answered in wild ways and two free spirits found their matching hearts.

First, I wrote this book (with open and sometimes shaking hands) to shout from my rooftop how *good*, merciful, and gracious our God is. And to tell the world how desperately He wants you to know Him and ask Him to write your life and love stories. He is not a God who forces us into anything. Oh no, He is a God of grace, gentleness, and patience. He doesn't want puppets and playthings, but desires real relationship with His children. He gives us each freedom to choose our life path: to fearlessly follow Him in faith, believe in Jesus, trust Him with our lives – and spend eternity in Heaven with Him. Or choose to deny Him: turn from Jesus, reject His help and good purposes – walking separately from Him and ultimately spending eternity apart from Him.

Second, I wrote to encourage and inspire you to know you are not alone, you are not crazy, and that you are not waiting and trusting in vain. It *is* hard but well worth every sacrifice. You are not "missing out" and you are not a dork. As a man and woman on the "other side" of the waiting journey, we want our still-waiting brothers and sisters to know it is oh so worth the wait! God is incredibly faithful to all His promises. It's gonna be worth it *all*!

And third, my heart behind writing this book is to give you hope, wherever you are, my friend. Your path and story may look totally different than mine. Maybe you're a teenage girl wondering what your life will look like and wrestling with longing for love. Perhaps you're a single lady who feels very, very forgotten. Maybe you're a married mama or a seasoned grandma who holds secret dreams in her heart and desires God to breathe life into them once again. Perhaps you've already lived two or three love stories and feel disenchanted and lost, like there's no hope or redemption left for you. Maybe you are in the middle of a sunny season and want to keep your eyes focused on Him. Maybe you are in a season of loss and darkness much like the times Daniel and I faced in our stories, and are struggling to believe that God is good. I want you to know I prayed over *every single one* of these pages that you would be inspired, encouraged, brought close to Jesus, and uplifted – wherever you are.

May my words give you hope. Fresh, new hope you've never tasted. Or awaken lost, forgotten hope.

And so, dear reader, go find a cozy nook in your couch, cuddle up with a soft throw, and pour yourself a cup of steamy coffee.

Open your heart to hope, again. I promise you – it's real and right there waiting for you.

Author's Note

In this book, I share my heart on paper. Our whole story. The untold parts. Far more than the bits and pieces shared on a few of my blog posts and short social media captions. The details. The ups and downs. The happiest *and* the saddest moments. And I didn't spare many details. Of course, there are parts of our story that are "ours," – sacred and special – and other parts that are not ours to tell. I want to be real and tell it all in a way that is true and honest, while carefully holding the pen in my hand like an egg, wary of dropping its fragile shell.

But it's all here: the good, the bad and the ugly. It isn't shiny and flawless, sensational or perfect. It isn't a Hollywood script with a movie star cast of characters, epic soundtrack and perfect fairytale ending. It's just a real life story full of brokenness. I could have easily (and was tempted to, at times) "leave out" certain things. It would read easier, make me look more godly, and be far less vulnerable. But I couldn't and still be in integrity with myself, God, and you, my very important reader.

At the same time, I do understand and take seriously that I hold a responsibility to my younger readers, who see us as role models, to be careful. Yet, I want you to know the real me. The real us. Not the glossed over, perfect-looking airbrushed versions – dressed in our buttoned-up Sunday best.

Our love story is not an example. This book is not a "10 steps to being perfect, having it all together, and doing A, B, and C to achieve your best life, perfect love story, and blessing from God." I don't want it to be viewed as a model "for a Godly relationship," or even the ever-popular Instagram comment, *"goals."* It is simply our life: our messy, broken, failing and trying, imperfect life. We are saved by grace. And all our choices and steps were not the one "perfect" model to follow. Our story is a testimony of God's grace and redemption, not about anything we have done.

Everything good in our lives comes from God, and we believe (and have seen with our eyes) that when you surrender to Him and give Him the authorship of your life and love stories, you get to watch Him make something absolutely beautiful out of the mess. It is God's grace in action. Only grace. He gives hope to the hopeless and places the lonely in families.

In full disclosure and out of a heart to be respectful and careful, note that some names have been changed to protect the privacy of certain individuals and some minor details and names of things have been altered.

This is the story. And gosh, we are grateful.

"For from His fullness we have all received, grace upon grace."
John 1:16

Part One

1,710 MILES AND 27 YEARS APART

Tacos, Sailboats, and One Big Baby

Once upon a time, there lived a funny and ambitious, curly-haired teenage boy who rode a 10 speed bike around a small town in sunny Southern California. His face was olive toned and chiseled. He had laughing eyes and a dimple in his chin. And he fell in love with a demure brunette who capably managed a Taco Bell restaurant on a busy street corner in the small suburb north of Los Angeles. His name was Jim Girdlestone, and when he applied for the job of taco fryer/bathroom cleaner/dish washer at her fine establishment, he was swiftly rejected. The pretty eighteen year-old brunette manager named Candy Wagner laughed in his face and tore up his application, throwing it away in the trash can along with greasy old beef. Chuckling to her co-workers, she flipped her hair and said, "That boy isn't a day over fourteen! He looks like a *baby*! And, Girdlestone…? That is *the* dumbest last name I have ever heard!"

Convinced he was far too young to legally work, she insisted she could not hire him. But day after day, he persisted — because that is who he is. Returning on his 10 speed bike, filling out application after application, begging to make tacos with that beautiful, aloof young woman. She wore a loosely fitting brown uniform she still describes as "frumpy." But in his eyes, then and now — thirty-five years later – it was nothing less than "hot."

Then one day, as the Lord would have it – on his sixty-fifth try – she happened to (happily, for him) be out of town on vacation. The manager in charge who took her place that week hired him, right off the bat.

When she returned to work after her time away, she found him — wild brown curls in a net and eyes dancing like waves in the sea — wearing an ugly brown apron and frying taco shells. She couldn't help but smile. He winked. He melted her coldness. He became her very best friend. They fell in love.

And the rest, as they say, is history!

Jim and Candy were married on May 14th, 1983 in Santa Clarita, California, madly in love with each other, and with the sea. Back in the Taco Bell days, they'd sit on the plastic counters in their little fast food kitchen, long after their co-workers clocked out and they'd talk and talk, well into the night, about their dreams. Always dreaming about the ocean. About buying a sailboat and sailing all around the world, wild and free — just the two of them. Soon, they saved up enough money to buy a little ocean beauty! Jim studied for his sailing license and Candy fit perfectly as his first mate. Oh, the trips they took and the fun they had. They kept their boat in a little slip at Ventura Harbor, close to our hometown, and on weekends, holidays, and whenever-they-could-days, they'd pack up their car and live and love on its sunny deck. They were dreamers, through and through. They dreamed of sailing around the world. And changing it, too.

Almost four years after their wedding day, in the crisp autumn of 1986 — just a few days before Thanksgiving, I entered the world, chubby cheeked and bald, weighing in at nearly ten pounds. Mom says I could hold my head up and stand up when held, more like a five month old at birth than a newborn! They sold their sailboat but kept their dreams. Mom taught piano lessons from our home and Dad — a brilliant writer — attended college and worked hard doing whatever he could to support his little family. They often talked of God and spiritual things, but they didn't know Him. Not yet, anyway. They didn't have a lot of money, but they were in love — no one could doubt it! And that would always be enough.

Mom gushed over her new little girl. I was colicky and cranky, but one very loved baby. She thoroughly enjoyed motherhood. She soaked up every single moment.

My very first childhood memory (and this is no lie —
although, Daniel highly questions my claim) is falling
asleep on Dad's chest the day they brought me home
from the hospital. We bonded that day.

Just a few months after I was born, Mom found out
they were expecting *another* little one! We took walks
every day to Penguins (the local frozen yogurt shop)
and I loved reading books. Seventeen months later,
Mandy May was born on a perfectly warm day in —
you guessed it — May.

A sister! A friend! I (a still semi-bald baby myself) was
simply thrilled.

She came home from the hospital as the birds chirped
and flowers bloomed. I remember Dot (our beloved
Mom's Mom) was folding wash cloths and towels on
the brown couch as she explained to me that Momma
was having a baby at the hospital and she would be
home soon.

Dad and Mom brought her home in a white carrier,
and I leaned over her scrunchy little face, kissed her
tiny forehead and from that day forward, we were the
of best friends.

Sweet Tea and Twins

Who knew that while romance and a little family
bloomed in Southern California, a love story brewed
like coffee in a percolator in Pine Bluff, Arkansas. All

the way across the map: one thousand, seven hundred and ten miles away.

While my parents flirted over fried taco shells, sailed the high seas of the Pacific, and rocked a baby girl in their arms, a devoted young pastor named Terry Morris met a young lady named Cindy Jones at church. He attended Ouachita Baptist University and she had her very own clothing shop.

She was exciting, pretty, and very hard to get. She had dark blonde hair and Terry could tell she was a nice, godly young woman. She'd just gotten saved and spent her weekends serving at the church.

All the young men at church chased her, unable to catch her eye or to catch a date. Terry just watched and laughed at them, not thinking a thing about Cindy. Because, you see, he was already committed to a girlfriend of his own.

The Lord presented an opportunity for Terry to travel to Nigeria as an exchange student and he took it. He spent six months studying in the foreign land, making lifelong memories. As the time wore on, he realized that he and his girlfriend back in Arkansas were growing distant. In a time when communication across continents consisted of simple hand-written letters rather than Internet, he wrote to her… their hearts had grown detached. He sealed it and posted it – Nigeria to the southern United States. But unbeknownst to him, she had written, sealed, and sent a letter too. The two letters crossed one another somewhere over the Atlantic. He opened it up, a few weeks later, reading her explanation. She met someone else. She moved on. She was engaged, in fact. And it was over.

It's funny how things don't work out.

And it's funny how they do.

He returned from Africa to Arkansas. And Cindy Jones immediately caught his eye. He fell for her, right off.

She accepted his invitation when he asked her on a date! Because, she saw something different in Terry from the other young men at church. Something good.

She drove that poor boy crazy. She seemed as though she liked him, a lot. He'd pursue more. And then she would draw back. She was a beautiful butterfly– and hard to pin down.

The two spent time together, went on many dates, and finally… they decided to get to it and tie that knot!

On a cool November day in Pine Bluff, they became husband and wife. Side by side, choosing and committing to faithfulness — to one another and to God, in whatever path He chose for them. From the very start, they mutually felt passionate about opening their hands, arms and home to all the children God saw fit to give them. They committed, wholeheartedly, to serve the Lord and build a strong, God-honoring family for Him, formed on a faithful partnership.

Ten months later, they welcomed not one but *two* sweet little babies! Perfect, tiny twin boys (who together weighed as much as I did at birth!) Caleb Neil, born first and Daniel Terry, born second.

Their parents tell the story.

Of how Caleb came out, all pink and screaming. And two minutes later, Daniel was born... white as a sheet, limp as a rag. The nurse wrapped him up in a blanket and the doctors whisked him away to another room, before his mama could even hold him. Caleb cried and kicked as they swaddled him, while Daniel lay still, silent and pale.

Daniel spent the first hours of his life in the NICU. His dad and mom still had not held their second sweet baby boy. It was heart wrenching and scary. They prayed, fervently, begging the Lord to spare their child, one they'd not yet even met and barely even seen. The whole family and church prayed, asking the Lord to spare him, to heal him.

Forty-eight hours later, he was released from the NICU into his young parent's loving and very grateful arms. The Lord spared his life, saved him, and healed him. Terry and Cindy breathed a sigh of relief as they swaddled the two squirming twins and brought them home. They were *especially* thankful they brought home *both* of them and that Daniel survived and was okay.

Little did they know, that in the years to come, the heart-stopping fear of losing their second born twin would haunt them, yet again.

A California Country Girl

I have never lived anywhere but California. The sunshine drenched, desert hills of So Cal — the west – has always been my home. I spent my early years in a small horse town in LA County called Acton, just south of the Mojave Desert and forty miles north of Los Angeles.

 Acton was a tiny, western-themed town. Most residents owned a small lot of land and almost everyone had at least one horse. We lived in a pale blue mobile home on Santiago Road. Dad landscaped a gorgeous yard and rock wall around it. I can still feel and smell the lush, dewy green grass under my feet as we hunted for Easter eggs every spring.

Dad worked as one of the head salesmen for Budweiser, delivering beer to bars and clubs, restaurants and stores all over Los Angeles.

Mom, a talented and well-honed musician, taught piano lessons from home every week on her baby grand piano. Students came and went, while she could still be home with us girls. Some days, she traded a lesson with a young girl student for babysitting.

Life was good. Days full of Barbie playing, bike riding, watching "Aladdin" or "The Little Mermaid" — sometimes more than once a day. Nights filled with peaceful sleeping on my little wooden bed on clean Sesame Street sheets, holding My Pretty Ponies by their neon hair.

My girlhood was safe and protected. Mom saw to that. And we were always provided for. Dad saw to that. He worked hard, a young man with a head full of dreams and adventure and a house full of responsibility and children.

Mandy and I spent our days mostly playing Barbies. Ken always drove Barbie around in the hottest of hot pink convertibles, and – for some unexplained reason, always and only wore a uniform of red Christmas boxer shorts with white candy canes dotting them. (Ken liked to keep things sexy – and festive, apparently.) I spent the next few years singing my favorite song: "Someday my prince will come, someday I'll find my love but for now it is only a dream."

I sang it over and over, again and again as a little girl. So repetitively that Mandy would yell, "Stop! I am so sick of that song, Sis!" But I kept on singing and dreaming of my own prince charming, my own candy cane shorts wearing Ken.

While Mom taught piano, one of her ten-year-old students babysat us girls three days a week. She was sweet and absolutely *crazy* about some guy named Jesus. That girl was on fire. And I remember — at the age of six — noticing. It made me stop and wonder.

She'd sneak a colorful children's Bible in her backpack when she came to babysit, along with a green flannel board. She read stories of Jesus to us, acting them out with the little felt figures. I learned all about Him, and something about Him made my heart feel very happy.

Mom and Dad did not know Him. Oh, they talked about "spiritual things." They wondered. They questioned. They hashed out ideas and theories, for hours and hours and hours, but they did not know Jesus and they did not believe. Dad — a voracious reader and "brain on legs" as I call him, and Mom — a deeply spiritually sensitive person with a huge heart and quietly racing mind, spent much of their time discussing spirituality. Truth. Right and wrong. God and gods.

And if they admitted it? They were really very confused.

They were on the hunt for truth. They just hadn't found it yet.

But, in the early autumn of 1992, as the leaves began to slowly turn and fall, life as I knew it began to change. Dad and Mom's marriage began to crumble.

An Oklahoma Cowboy

The little Morris family lived in Arkansas until the toe-headed twins were five. The town was small and their family was growing. Terry worked as youth pastor at their church and Cindy spent her time raising her babies. Two more joined the family: Bethany and Elijah, seventeen months apart.

Cindy's parents lived close by and Daniel remembers many summer days spent in their big blue pool, learning to swim like a little fish in the deep end.

In 1993, a church plant in Oklahoma offered Terry a job as head pastor. The growing family packed up their life, kissed their beloved grandparents goodbye, and moved to start a new season in a tiny historic town in the heart of Oklahoma called Guthrie.

Daniel spent his formative years on Oak Street. Their new house was little and made of red bricks and brown siding. Daniel, his twin companion, and their younger siblings – little Anna now joining the group – played in the small backyard. Running wild outside, climbing the big pine tree, and finding bird nests.

He loved riding bikes all over their neighborhood street. Daniel vividly recalls biking down the hill really fast one summer afternoon, heading straight for a big truck parked on the side of the road. His brakes didn't work quickly enough and he smashed head-first into the truck. Scared and shaking, he was instructed by Mom and Dad that he needed to walk down the hill and explain to the truck's owner what happened. To offer an apology. Six-year-old Daniel trembled but obeyed.

This how he was raised from the beginning: to do the right thing and to be honest.

Every Sunday, the family of now-seven, loaded up in the Station Wagon and went to church to sit in a line in the pew and listen to Dad preach. Hearing truth upon truth every weekend soaked into Daniel's young soul.

On February 14th of 1993, Daniel woke up and worked on school at the kitchen table. His mind and heart were full lately, thinking on Dad's sermons; about Jesus, about his own heart, and about his sin.

All the Bible reading, sermons, the family prayer times at night, and the day in – day out example of his parents – sank into his young soul and he could not help but respond.

That morning, as he closed his spelling book, he decided to talk to Mom about all this. He found her lying on the couch and he sat beside her.

He quietly looked at her and explained, in his little boy words, how he felt convicted of his sin. Dad preached all those sermons full of truth and he'd been thinking about it.

"Mom, I wanna get saved next Sunday and get baptized," he said, blue eyes wide.

"Getting saved" in his six-year-old mind involved church and baptism. His mama smiled and explained, "You don't have to wait to until next Sunday… you can do it now!"

And so she took him into her quiet room in the back of the house and explained the Gospel to her son. She led him in a prayer: asking the Lord to come into his heart and to forgive him of his sin.

Joy and peace washed over him. He was free! He was new! His eyes still light up – twenty-one years later – when he remembers that moment. "Man, I felt so good. It was powerful." The Lord was with him and His Holy Spirit in him… he knew it! He felt incredibly happy and full of joy! Life would never be the same again.

It was Valentine's Day. And his heart was truly filled with love!

"Therefore, if anyone is in Christ, the new creation has come:
The old has gone, the new is here!"
– 2 Corinthians 5:17

Troll Dolls, Poppyseed Muffins, and Jesus

Back in California, Mom and Dad separated for a few months. Some of Mom's piano students were from Christian families and a few of the moms noticed her sadness. She shared with them the struggles in her marriage and her heartache. They prayed with her on the piano bench, and told her their women's bible study group would be praying, daily, for restoration of our family.

One rainy night, a few weeks later, an unexpected knock sounded at the door. In the pouring rain, Dad stood – wet and weeping. Last night he had a dream. He wanted to come home, to come back to his wife and family.

The Lord began to rebuild our family, and we hadn't even met Him yet.

Dad and Mom realized together that they needed help from God.

They searched around and we visited several different churches. I remember how they all seemed stuffy, unfriendly, and like their noses were turned down on us.

One summer Sunday, Dad and Mom packed us girls up in the black Jeep Cherokee and took us to a new church a friend recommended. It was a laid-back place full of rickety round tables and chairs. The church met at the town's fair grounds and served coffee, lemonade from powder, and sticky Costco poppy seed muffins. It looked more like a dimly lit coffee shop than a church. People wore jeans and sneakers, and didn't care if you were dressed up fancy or not. I remember, the place felt special. Free. We heard the Gospel that Sunday. We all stood up together when the pastor gave an altar call, and we received salvation.

On August, 14th, 1993 – Jesus saved us. He saved me.

Dad went into Budweiser the next morning and quit.

Done with that scene, he walked out. Bravely. In faith. The very first step in a very radical life of faith my parents would and *still* lead to this day; one that requires great sacrifice and risk-taking. But it is worth it…for Him.

In the months that followed, we lost everything. Literally.

But my parents smiled more. And they were happy. And so was I.

People sometimes ask me, "How do you *know* you were saved at that age? You were so young." But, oh I knew and Daniel knew, as well. You know when you fall in love. You know when you've been rescued. You know when your life changes. I could feel it. I could feel Him. I could almost feel His breath on me at church when they would dim the lights and play soft, sweet songs to Him. I could sense Him whispering to me through every little thing. He was real and He was there.

"Jesus said, 'Let the little children come to me, and do not hinder them. For the kingdom of heaven belongs to such as these." – Matthew 19:14.

On Monday after we got saved, I asked Mom for one of those big, black trash bags. Without a word, I walked down the hall to my messy bedroom and began slowly but purposefully throwing things away. Mom tip-toed into the room, puzzled – asking what on earth I was doing. I explained, "Throwing everything away that Jesus wouldn't want me to have."

Funny, looking back, even small children know darkness when they see it. *"Now the Lord is the Spirit, and where the Spirit of the Lord is, there is freedom." 2 Corinthians 3:17.* I didn't own anything you'd think of as inherently evil, but remembering now how I felt then, I know some of things I possessed were not "freedom bringing" things. I threw away green-haired troll dolls, witch costumes I wore for dress-up, scary kid's movies and music. I remember feeling so very free, so alive, and so happy.

I didn't fully understand what it meant that day, I couldn't. What it would mean to be a Christian, the precious blessings of being one of His, and the cost of walking with Him that is very real, too. But I knew enough to know one thing very, very clearly: He loved me.

And I loved Him.

Today, if I look back into old keepsake boxes of childhood things from that time, I am sure to find my childish scribbles on anything I could write on. With phrases like: "Jesus loves you!" and "God is love!"

After Dad left Budweiser, he worked several jobs, striving faithfully to make ends meet. We were swept up into that big church at the fairgrounds. We spent 3-4 nights a week at church and as a baby Christian with a big heart for Jesus, Dad began leading the church's men's ministry. He dove head-first into ministry from day-one, and never turned back. Along with working like crazy and spending spare time at church, Dad worked hard at finishing college, studying to be a pastor.

Those were very lean years, but full of the things that mattered. At times we had very little. Money was hard to come by. People from church sometimes left groceries on our doorstep and someone gave us a car. But those lean times never bothered me.

Because we had Him.

And He was enough.

Mom and Dad prayerfully chose to homeschool. Unbeknownst to us, my young future husband and his family out in Oklahoma chose the very same way of schooling.

Today, it is quite common to be homeschooled. But in the very early 90's it was definitely *not* the norm, and even a bit taboo. Our parents were true pioneers and despite criticism from mostly everyone, felt the Lord strongly leading them to homeschool. The greatest part about homeschooling was how our mamas knew each of us so well – our strengths and weaknesses, our developing passions and personalities – and they designed our schooling for us, out of their hearts of faith and desire to raise us according to the Bible.

Hard Work, Character, and Music Notes

Daniel's brothers and sisters multiplied, quickly, and he became "big brother" to a little army of a family. His dad pastored the church in Guthrie for two years and when his ministry there came to a close, he moved on to work at Sara Lee Coffee and Tea in Oklahoma City. The family walked through lean times in that season with mouths to feed and bills to pay, babies to diaper and children to care for. His parents worked hard to provide for their family in those rough times.

The year Daniel turned six, his grandpa "Paps" helped the Morris family purchase a farm right outside Guthrie. How thrilling for a boy! Eighteen whole acres of cedar trees and scrubby brush… and perfect places to explore! Things to see! Mischief to get into! Adventures to have!

Seventeen acres became twenty-seven when "Pop," his grandpa on the other side, purchased ten acres behind the property, which is now dubbed "the back pasture." Oh what fun!

The family set up a cozy little home in that farmhouse which included a brown upright piano. It was ancient and out of tune, but the twins didn't mind – they took to it like flies to honey! Daniel and Caleb played that piano daily. They taught themselves. When they were six their mom bought them Alfred books and they went through them, daily and methodically, practicing without being told, studying the notes, learning the notation and playing "Row Your Boat" a thousand times a week.

Days were filled with homeschool, piano, chores, helping to care for babies, and running wild on the farmland.

Daniel began to learn classical pieces on the piano and practiced for hours every day. Music penetrated into his soul, and it changed him forever.

The farm now dubbed "Shekinah Springs Farm" (which means "God's Glory") saw several new arrivals join the fun: Molly the horse, Dakota the mare, a couple of cows, some pigmy goats, a few ducks, several turkeys, a variety of chickens, some cats, a few dogs, and best of all, a couple more brothers: Micah and then a little later, Andrew!

Those boyhood years were full of innocent play, fun and learning. Daniel was safe and sheltered on the farm. Music flowing through his veins, red Oklahoma dirt on his skin, a BB gun in his hand, a cowboy hat on his head, boots on his feet, and a bare back horse beneath him, a bunch of siblings to play with, and Jesus in his heart. Really, all a boy could ask for!

Now twelve, his relationship with the Lord grew, his understanding of faith blossomed, and his parents did their best to be sure they reared a godly young man.

Every night after he and his siblings were in their bunk beds, Terry came into their rooms for his nightly ritual. He laid his hand on Daniel's head (and each of the children alike) and gave him a blessing: "May the Lord bless you and keep you. May His face shine upon you and give you peace."

Daniel was taught, by example and in word, to honor God, treat women with respect, and to prepare his heart and mind for loving a wife someday. Now a big family of ten, every night the Morris family gathered in the living room to read scripture and pray. And the newest addition- baby Josh. Terry and Cindy prayed every night for their eldest sons, "That the Lord would bring them godly wives, in the right time."

Nightly, Daniel slipped away from the noise and constant busyness of their full home and spent a few moments in the boys' bedroom closet. He knelt to his knees within the tiny four walls where guns, bows, and arrows hung, and he prayed for his future wife.

He prayed that the Lord would bring him a wife in His time.

A godly wife.

He prayed that she would be protected and safe. He now remembers: "I prayed that the Lord would keep her… for me."

Church and a close-knit homeschool group became the family's community. At thirteen years old, Daniel saw a trio play at church —two violins and a cello. He and Caleb decided they wanted to learn a new instrument and chose violin.

The Ranch: Crown of the Valley

If you were a bird and you spread your wings wide and flew higher, higher, higher into the sky, over mountains and valleys, rivers and deserts, you would finally reach the foothill peaks of epic Southern California.

You would fly over a mountain and stop just seventy-five miles before reaching the deep blue Pacific Ocean. Flapping your wings, you would swoop down over big, old oak trees and rolling hills dotted with cows in pastures – until you reached a ranch. First, you'd notice wide fields and horses of every shade and color. Oak trees hung with simple rope swings. A long white fence stretching for acres: three-hundred-and-fifty, to be exact. And there you would be at the Ranch. *My ranch.* Rancho Corona Del Valle, Spanish for "Crown of the Valley."

You might gasp when you see how big and beautiful it is. I did. Welcome, my friend to my favorite place in the world. The place where I grew up. *The place where I fell in love with Jesus.*

When our family lost everything, we moved into a rental house on Avocado Lane. I had my own room. I hung sunflower printed curtains in the window. Mom sewed them for me. I remember singing along to Jars of Clay and Amy Grant tapes every afternoon, feeling oh so cool at the age of ten. The house wasn't fancy or even nice but we didn't care. It was set in an old neighborhood in a small town called Palmdale. Those were such happy, contented days filled with learning, long playdates with friends, many hours of Barbie and doll playing, watching "Little House on the Prairie" episodes, and playing piano and singing.

Even then, I was a country girl – I just didn't know it yet. My heart craved playing outside in the fresh air. Sometimes in the late afternoon while Mom made dinner, Mandy and I put on dress-up clothes and imagined we were Mary and Laura Ingalls. We ran around the backyard, pretending our two dogs were our horses and digging up the grass for our make-believe prairie gardens.

One summer evening as the sun slowly sank on our backyard play, Mandy removed her calico bonnet as Mom called us in for dinner. "Dad's at night school so let's eat our spaghetti now!"

As night set in and dinner served, the sound of a helicopter's propellers echoed outside our windows. We didn't think much of it – helicopters and police chases were not unheard of in this part of town. But as we ate our spaghetti and then washed the dishes, the helicopter noise remained, joined by a cop car siren….and then two, three, four, five sirens ringing, just outside. Mom peeked out our living room window and gasped: police cars lined and filled our entire cul-de-sac street! Red and blue lights lit up the living room as the helicopter sounds became closer, louder.

It was right above our house.

"Girls…. get down." Mom whispered, firmly. All three of us ducked behind the long couch. I remember shaking in fear. Mom prayed aloud, asking the Lord to protect us in the midst of whatever was going on outside. She led us to my bedroom in the back of the house, feeling it was safer than the open front room. As we walked in to huddle behind my bed for safety, we noticed a bright and unusual light shining through my window. The whirring buzz of the helicopter directly above our house was so very loud, it hurt my ears. I crept on my hands and knees on the carpeted floor, over to the window and slowly pulled back my sunflower printed curtains. Fear itself gripped my little heart as I saw a huge white helicopter hovering just above our backyard, its bright beam pointing at our backyard wall, light pouring directly onto a dark figure.

Someone was hiding in our backyard.

A man stood, pressed up against our backyard wall, not ten feet across the yard. As I looked through the glass and screen, he stared me directly in the eye and motioned over his mouth for me to be quiet.

I fell to the floor and whispered in a frantic, hysterical scream: *"Mom…there's a man up against the wall!"*

We never learned what happened that night. Mom called the police and the man in our backyard was gone when we looked out the window again. Dad rushed home from class and instructed Mandy and I to stay indoors, from now on. No playing outside without him, at all – ever. Our neighborhood was just too dangerous. My heart sank. No more playing outside. No more make-believe. No more digging in the dirt.

And to this day, I can't help but shiver a little at the sound of a helicopter.

The next morning as we sat down at the kitchen table with Mom, she placed her hands on our schoolbooks and said, "Girls, I know it's sad that you can't play outside anymore, but Dad says it's not safe when we are here alone." We didn't argue, last night's scare still chilling in our hearts. "But, I have an idea. Why don't we start praying and asking God to give us a new home! A safe home. We could pray every day together and ask Him. We could write a list of things we dream of. We can ask Him for anything! Why not? He can do it!"

"Girls, *He can do anything.*"

So, we took our pens to paper and wrote a list. Just like Mom suggested. A list of dreams. Of things we wanted in a new home. And it went like this:

"Lord, I pray that You would give us a home that has:

- Safety
- A pool
- A tree house
- A safe place to play outside
- Land and dirt to dig in
- Friends to meet
- Swings
- A place for animals

I prayed through the list every day with the unflinchingly firm faith of an innocent child's soul, believing my God could do *anything.* I never once doubted He wanted good things for me, not because I thought He was like Santa Claus, but because I knew He was my Father.

A few months later, the door to the year 1998 opened. I was twelve. And God answered our prayers.

He answered them in a way I could never have imagined; an "above and beyond" kind of way. I saw it before my eyes, for the first time ever in my young life: His ability to do immeasurably more than all we ask or imagine, according to His power that is at work within us (*Ephesians 3:20*). I saw that His plan is better than anything I could ever imagine, dream up or make happen without Him.

"Are not two sparrows sold for a penny? Yet not one of them will fall to the ground outside your Father's care. And even the very hairs of your head are all numbered. So don't be afraid; you are worth more than many sparrows." Matthew 10:29-31

The pastor of our church called Dad. He offered him a job: Director of the Ranch School of Ministry, a beautiful place hidden in the hills. The Ranch was owned by a kind, successful family who were part of founding the legendary Hollywood Bowl. Through a series of God-ordained events, twenty years before, our church worked out a deal: they cared for the Ranch in exchange for use of it. The arrangement worked out perfectly for both parties. The Ranch was staffed by godly people and they hosted schools full of students from all over the world who (in faith) chose to leave their countries and homes for a place in California. The Ranch (much like a YWAM school) grew organically out of prayer and hearts for Jesus, all by simple word of mouth over twenty-five years.

The nations came to that mountain, people from almost every country in the world and it became known simply as "The Ranch" by the people who loved it.

The Ranch, to me, felt magical, like a fairyland, a special place. Not a Disneyland kind of magical but more of a Heavenly kind of magical. Something hung in the air over that place. It felt sacred…special. A haven in the midst of the desert, tucked away in the safe cove of a mountain, surrounded by tall, protective pine trees, rolling dry fields of golden grass, and dotted with old, old oak trees. The place was dedicated in prayer to the Lord – a place where people came to spend undistracted time with God without televisions, the responsibilities of their normal lives, nor the disruption of the Internet.

I'll never forget my first visit to the Ranch.

We drove up the dirt road, lined with a white fence. Chestnut brown and dirty white horses with bleach blonde manes galloped in grassy fields inside. Fat brown cows lazily chomped on weeds on the other side. It was beautiful, homey, rustic and real. Everything you would imagine a classic California working horse ranch to be, complete with dusty roads, broken fences, big horses, chickens, and a goat. It was charmingly vintage: a cross between thoroughly country and delightfully "cowboy".

We walked up and down the paths to explore it all and drink it up, starting at the entrance gate where cows grazed all day long in their pens. On my left, a huge, grand, white wooden barn stood wide and long.

The Ranch Manager walked us through the dark inside. It smelled like rotten wood and wet hay. He told us that Clark Gable kept his horses here while he filmed movies in Los Angeles. Rumor has it that when his beloved wife, Carole Lombard, was killed in a plane crash in 1942, Clark mourned over her, fiercely. He found his only solace in coming to the Ranch, mounting his horses, and riding for hours alone on the desolate, rugged paths of those wide acres.

On a hill above the white barn, two paths diverged, leading to several plain but quaint homes. This is where my family would live!

Up a very steep dirt path above it all was "The Reservoir" – a huge sparkling blue and seemingly infinite, deep pool, fed by crisp, clean natural springs on the mountain and surrounded by pine trees. The view from the water was gorgeous, like a panoramic painting, the ranch sprawled out below all picturesque and quiet, with the Mojave Desert floor below.

Down the steep dirt road again, I remember coming upon five cabins. This is where the students lived. They were painted pale blue with white trim and affectionately called "The Cottages" by one of the British ladies. Quite honestly, they looked to me as though they belonged somewhere on the East Coast in Cape Cod or a moor somewhere in England, rather than on a rustic California horse ranch. Inside, the cottages smelled like lumber and were carefully decorated. Cottage #1 was instantly my favorite, because of its cozy rose throw pillows, bedding in a white and pink rose spray pattern, white wicker furniture, flowers everywhere, a cozy little loft above, and pink carpet (which sounds tacky but for this place, it totally worked). Many girlhood memories would be formed there – slumber parties with Mandy and close friends; and many life-altering prayers would be prayed in that little cottage. But I did not know it yet.

On a slope below was a grassy lawn with chairs looping around a fire pit and a building with a sign that read "Classroom." Next to that was a one-hundred-year old house with a fireplace, converted into offices and rooms for students, and a small building painted red that served as the Ranch school's kitchen.

Below was the Ranch owner's Spanish adobe style mansion, built in the early 1900's. It looked like it might fit more comfortably on a sunny street in Santa Barbara. A gigantic oak tree towered high above the land around the mansion – the Ranch Manager told us that Kit Karson slept in the tree during his travels to California gold country. I believed it.

Tucked beside the long driveway leading up to the mansion was a pine tree covered cove. I was drawn there immediately. There was a swing and a bench surrounded by a rustic wood picket fence. Winding through the middle was a path filled with the intoxicating scent of pine needles, which reminded me of Christmas. It was like a secret garden. Mandy and I named it "Lover's Lane" and Mom would soon read to us from "Anne of Green Gables" as we sat under the shady pine trees.

I hopped into the back bed of an old, dirty, beat-up Chevrolet truck with Mandy. Mom and Dad rode in the front. The ranch manager drove us all around those dirt roads.

Spring was in the air, cold but not biting. I vividly remember the sky above was gray, with the afternoon light shining desperately through the clouds. I saw mist hanging in the air as we rode in the truck bed, wind whipping my hair all around my smiling face. Mist mingled with the green and gold leaves in the oak trees, hiding in the corners of the brush and wildflowers, giving the place the appearance of a mysterious, heavenly fairy land that I thought belonged perched on a cloud somewhere, far above earth.

This place was unlike anywhere I had ever seen!

I realized, then and there: that every single thing on my prayer list came true at the Ranch.

Everything I prayed for, He gave.

Tree house? Check. And not just a tree house. An old-fashioned, huge, gorgeous *house* built perched in the big branches of a one hundred-and-fifty-year-old oak tree. With little windows, a deck, and a big room it was the mother of all tree houses, I tell you.

Swings? Not just swings. Oh, no. There was a swing set near the owner's mansion. But even better? The tree house tree held the most wonderful, long, dreamy rope swing on earth! I felt like I was flying when I slipped inside the knot and soared over the hill.

A pool? Not just a normal pool. A sparkling, big, blue, deep as the ocean (to my little girl eyes) swimming hole, where we would soon spend countless hours splashing in its little fresh-spring waterfall and basking in the sunshine.

Dirt to play in? Three hundred and fifty acres of it, thank you very much.

And the list went on and on.

Every single prayer, every single item on that list made with mom the day after fear struck and we stepped up in faith to ask God to give us a safe, good home?

Answered.

And not only answered? But answered, specifically.

Ten fold.

Undeniably. In my face! It blew me away.

We moved to the Ranch in the summer of 1998, my twelfth year.

The first night in our new gift-from-God ranch home, I remember Dad opened the big, wide window above my bed. Finally, all was well. It was safe. The cool, fresh air wafted in my window through the screen, thick with the fragrance of dried hay and the unmistakable, intoxicating scent of damp sagebrush. I can almost smell it now, and will never forget it. I smiled as I laid my head on the blue floral pillow, whispering praise to Him. I drifted into a peaceful sleep. Finally home, where I belonged.

Those days were laced with happiness.

Not a temporal or circumstantial happiness because God answered my prayer for a new home. Not because every single detail, wish, and thought on my prayer list had been answered, to a "T" – in an almost uncanny way. Those things were fingerprints of His gracious hand. But the happiness came from simply knowing, seeing, and tasting how *good* He is.

For the first time in my young life, I saw how *specific* God is. How intimately He knows us. How personal He is. How He fashioned us purposefully and knows our hearts. How He created our desires and cares about our dreams. All the answered prayers were so clearly from His hand, and it was undeniable.

I was undone that summer. His extravagant love wrecked me, starting then and continuing through the years that followed.

He ruined me for anything else. Anything less.

One thing I saw and knew: the happiness came from *Him*…just being Him. Being near, being present, and being faithful.

There was soul-warming joy in finding His peace, feeling His presence, and walking in His freedom. In being truly free to laugh, to dance, to shine, to learn, to sing, to grow, to worship, to run. Free to bloom. Free to ask and speak. Free to be bold. Free to love.

The sweetness of that season taught me the beautiful truth that God is not a heavy-handed judge who looks down on us with penalizing eyes, like some kind of referee. He is not an intimidating police officer who chases us down when we screw up and writes out a ticket to punish us every time we make a mistake. He is not some weird version of Santa Claus who sits up in the clouds, looking down at us disapprovingly, shaking His head as He puts us on the "Naughty List" for the year. No, He is far from the images we so often get into our heads about Him.

My dear reader, I found Him at the Ranch. I could almost see Him, feel Him, taste Him. I met Him through a thousand little things and fell head over heels in love with Him.

In all I learned and saw of Him, I found that – above all – He is a lover.

It was a unique and very privileged way to grow up. I witnessed a parade of souls from all over the planet come in and out of my life at The Ranch – for years people came from every country and nation, and every walk of life – who spoke all different languages and had vastly different life experiences. And yet, they all knew Him. How could they all know Him if He wasn't real? I saw Him in the faces of the students and teachers from the nations. He became so evident to me in those years. He was nearly tangible. It wasn't about churchiness, legalism, or following a set of rules, or looking a certain way, but a real, tangible relationship with the living God. One that I could see and feel and taste — just being around them. It was intoxicating. And I wanted it, too.

And I fell in love, hard.

Those days and years were full to the brim with life. They were charmed. I didn't realize then that shadows would soon fall, and clouds would surely darken the sunny skies above us.

Brokenness cannot help but find us. We are weak, fragile humans who need help, rescue…a savior. Knowing Him before the winter came and the iciness of life we all face at one time or another nearly froze me: It made all the difference.

Part Two

I'LL BE WAITING

The Jordan River and A Future Husband

"There is a baptism at church next month," dad told me as we stood at the kitchen counter at home, filling taco shells with beef, cheese and lettuce (our family's signature meal, as you might have guessed). "Do you want to get baptized?"

I thought for a moment. Mom and Dad had asked me before. Many times. I was twelve, ready, and understood the act of baptism. But no, I'd already decided while reading the Gospels last year. I'd read how Jesus was baptized in the Jordan River in the nation of Israel… and, at the time, I asked the Lord if I could be baptized, for the first time, where He was.

"No. Not yet."

Dad smiled.

"I know, I know – you want to get baptized in the Jordan River, like Jesus. Okay."

It sounded crazy, I admit. But, I knew how big and good He was. Even though I was a pastor's kid with absolutely no money of my own and no hope of a plane ticket to Israel in sight, I believed. And more importantly, I prayed. As they always did, Mom and Dad supported and believed along with my big, crazy dreams and prayers.

The next day after lunch, I raced down to the mailbox at the entrance to The Ranch and popped the metal cover open. All the mail for the students was in a rubber band… and there was a little white box. *It was here!* I let out a squeal and ran up the hill to our house.

Almost thirteen years old, my biggest life dream was to be married, someday. I was still just a little girl, really, but somehow, my heart already belonged to the man I would marry. I read books and listened to songs about waiting. Appropriately, I didn't really fully understand what sex was, but I knew it was sacred, meant for marriage, and between husband and wife. And, I knew I was going to choose to save it for my husband someday.

Somehow, I was sure. That beautiful man? Well, he was out there, waiting for me, too.

I was the teenager who asked her parents for a purity ring. They didn't know what it was and they certainly didn't force it on me. They always supported my commitment and it was born out of the values they taught me. But it was all me. All my idea. Inspired by His word.

I prayed, and wrote in my journal: "Lord, I want one man. One man only. And I want *You* to pick 'him' out."

The waiting began.

Mandy and I spent those summer days running around the rolling hills with our best friend, Rachel. We sang and made up songs and games. We laughed and dressed up in make-believe.

It was an innocent, simple time, full of faith and pure, naïve play. I became obsessed with music, along with Mandy. Every chance we could, we sang to tracks of our favorite Point of Grace songs. We adored harmonizing together and absolutely lived for music.

We spent many summer nights having slumber parties in the pink Cottage #1, with Rachel. When the sky went black and the stars came out, we three young girls tip toed out onto the sprawling green lawn and sat in a circle. We'd hold hands and bow our heads. And one by one, we would pray for our future husbands. Oh how we'd giggle and talk about who they'd be, how they'd look, and what our lives would be like someday.

We practiced this ritual almost weekly: giving God our dreams, hopes, and future husbands.

Another dream cropped up in our hearts… something sort of random, but beautiful, all the same. Rachel had started Irish dance lessons, and we often awkwardly copied her moves. It inspired in us an idea – we decided our newest, biggest dream was to someday travel to Ireland together. It was wild. Our families had meager incomes and the thought of an overseas trip to Europe was all but impossible and outlandishly silly, really. But, with young and unbroken hearts full of faith and eyes full of dreams, we added "An Ireland Trip" to our prayer list, as well. We'd pray and pray, every sleepover and slumber party, along with our pizza and nail polish. Our God was big and He was good. And we trusted Him.

Well-known pastors, worship leaders, missionaries and speakers came to The Ranch in those years. Our family's very favorite worship leader, Rita Springer, visited that autumn. She gave prophetic words to the students in the cozy classroom. One afternoon, she broke down weeping as she prayed for me and Mandy. She told us sacred, earth shattering things. That He loved us. That life would not always be easy, but He would be there. That we were His girls and we were especially anointed and called to do big things for Him.

She said He told her that even though she had no idea if we could sing, He wanted her to ask us to sing backup for her that night at the big worship service at church. We were honored, and singing along with her – in her desperate love for Him, undid me.

I was on a frantic search to find the hem of His garment and know Him more.

A few months later, Dad came home with some exciting news: he'd been asked to lead a church tour trip to Israel, of all places…and our family? Invited to go along with him.

He looked me in the eyes, and said, smilingly "Your dream may come true, after all."

I was over the moon thrilled!

I'll never forget driving up the hill as a golden sun set into Jerusalem. The place where Jesus walked, the very dirt. It blew my young mind. Tears streamed down my cheeks as our bus journeyed up and over the hill…and there it was, in all its glory. Just as I'd read in my Bible.

One hot dry day in August, in the Holy Land, the Lord answered my prayer. I'd prayed it, wide eyed and expectant, with nothing in sight that made me think it could ever possibly come true.

I was baptized in the big green Jordan River, in the nation of Israel. Sparkling in the sunlight.

Just as He promised; just as I imagined. It was absolutely wonderful. That moment and on that whole ten-day trip, He was alive and real and right beside me.

During those years, Dad continued to direct and lead the Ranch, while also being asked to pastor at the big church where we were saved. Mom played piano on the worship team. Soon, Mandy and I were asked to join the worship team as well. After singing with Rita and performing at a church talent show, the worship pastor saw our passion for music. Suddenly, our family became integral to every church service. I sang with Mandy almost every Sunday. Mom played piano. Dad often preached. We lived life in the "ministry fish bowl" and I just adored the community (and the attention, quite honestly). We sang, in harmony. The church's congregation was about 4,000, and classified as a "mega church." When we sang, people wept. When we led worship under the bright shining lights, on the huge high stage, thousands of people felt His presence. They told us, every Sunday. It was humbling and heady, flattering and overwhelming for a teenager to absorb. On a small scale, Mandy and I became little "celebrities" in our church. People asked for our autograph, and stood in line to talk to us every Sunday. They wrote on bulletins how they felt God when we sang and slipped them in the offering basket. They pushed our friends out of the way when they wanted to hug us after worship service, heartbreakingly. Music became my life. And I had an absolute ball: four services per weekend I got to sing my little heart out (with a full on rock band) in a congregation of the people I loved the most. I felt close to the Lord when I worshipped. Those were full and happy days. Full to the brim of dreams come true. People often told me, "You will be famous someday! You girls are just so good."

But I remember one particular Sunday when a kind lady I knew had been through some very rough stuff in life, took me aside after service. She had tears in her eyes as she held onto my hand and told me that as I sang, the Lord put some things on her heart. She saw me on stages, leading worship in the future. She saw me writing and speaking to women. Then, she told me this:

"The Lord wants you to know....that life will not always be peaches and cream. But He will *always, always, always* be with you."

It scared me, a little. But soon, as the years would unfold and shadows fell, I'd hold onto her words, closely.

During that season, our family moved from The Ranch to a property down the street – Dad and Mom bought twenty-eight acres of classic California wilderness and built a gorgeous, craftsman style house. Their heart behind investing in the land and home was that it would be an inheritance for their children someday.

My family became closer with a young man in those years. His name was Justin. Dad mentored him and he spent many times at our family's home and with us at church. We took a half-week long sailing trip with him to the Channel Islands. He was very tall and kind and smart and godly. The first and only mature young man of God I'd ever become friends with, really. And in my innocent and unbroken girlish heart, I became absolutely sure – beyond a shadow of a doubt – that he was my future husband. I was positive. The Lord had given me signs and shown me things, I believed. This was it. This was him. God could do anything and He could do this. Eight years my senior, I would need to grow up a bit, of course. I looked up at him with big heart eyes. I felt sure. He was "the one."

Oh, the woes of unrequited love. Especially on a young woman's heart.

Violins and Prayers

At the tender age of fifteen, Daniel Morris decided that dating was not for him. He desired to be undistracted. The homeschool group their family was in encouraged "courtship" rather than "dating" and so he followed suit. He continued praying for his future wife, longing to be married someday. The rest of his time he poured into music.

The Morris family had grown all the more in the past few years of life on the farm. Jeremiah joined the family in our absence, and next, Hosanna!

In the fall of 2002, Daniel's parents discovered they were expecting baby number eleven....and *twelve*! Twins *again*! Two bouncing boys: Josiah and Joel. And this time? Their two eldest twins were put to work. Daniel spent many an evening rocking and burping, feeding and changing the new set of twins.

He adored them both, but he and Joel developed a very special bond. They became best friends. That little guy was his kindred spirit from day one! The family called him "Bally" for his round, bald head, and he followed his big brother Daniel around everywhere he went.

In those years, Daniel's heartbeat didn't sound like a thud... it sounded like a violin's sad, soft voice, and sometimes, a piano.

Days and nights were filled with music, school, and running around the back pasture wearing a coonskin cap and making elaborate home movies with his siblings.

Daniel had a very wholesome upbringing on the farm. Life was about family, church, faith, knowing God and growing into a good, strong man who worked hard. Early mornings and late nights were spent playing violin. And in between he swept floors and helped calm crying babies. It was the perfect mix of a character-building upbringing. My man was getting ready for his destiny.

Belfast, Ireland.

October, 2003.

Rain pattering on the thatched rooftop of a square house. Inside, a warm firelight glows. A grey-haired woman pours English breakfast tea from a shiny, antique silver tea pot. I take the cup in my hand and stir in a few sugar cubes.

Ireland.

The prayer came true! Rachel, Mandy, and I along with Mom and Dad, were given the opportunity to spend three weeks in Ireland, serving and doing some ministry as Dad preached in churches.

The Lord answered the prayers of three little girls.

He is kind.

My eyes had seen radical, wild-eyed prayers answered in swift, effortless touches of His hand. I could have sworn, more times than the years that added up my age, that He answered very *specific* and big as the sky dreams. He listened to His children. And He cared, oh so much. About the big, life altering things. And about the little things too.

My faith, strong. I'd seen it. I'd seen Him. How could I deny? How could I not believe? And if my God, who I'd seen and felt, cared about where I lived, got baptized, and parts of the world I longed to see with my best friends, then surely He cared about the life I would lead, the path I would take, and the man I would marry.

I prayed and prayed, daily, hourly, for "my man." My journal... full of prayers and hopes.

Specific requests.

I prayed for a gentleman.

I prayed for a man of integrity. Gentleness. Purity and honor. Strength and valor. A man like Jesus.

With a dictionary in hand, a concordance, my Bible and my journal, I'd often sit down for hours and pray on a specific character topic. That the Lord would move and work on my heart and my future husband's, whoever he may be, out there in the world.

I prayed, daily.

That he would be tall and lean but strong.

I begged that he would *please* have blue eyes?

Light hair.

A heart of gold.

That he would love music and be a musician. And more importantly, a worshipper.

I prayed that he would love children, and want to have a family.

That he would be sweet. And strong. A man of stellar character and self-control. A man who respected women. The women in his life, his mom and sisters.

I prayed that, while young, he would be kept from dating too much and would be more focused on the Lord and his calling.

I prayed that he would be a good, servant-hearted man of God.

I always imagined and prayed for my dream man and his dreamy proposal to me: my future husband, on bended knee, asking me to marry him by the sea and crashing waves, with a pink sun setting. It would be magic.

Sitting in the big parlor in Belfast, sipping my tea, I listened to Dad preach. He was ministering that day to a group of leaders and pastors, encouraging them in their ministries. I sat, taking in his talk on Abraham and Isaac. How desperately Abraham desired Isaac. How the Lord finally gave him. But then, how He asked for Abraham to give him up. To surrender him – the dream – the love. And to trust God.

Dad instructed all of us in the room to sit as a worship song played, and to ask the Lord what our "Isaac" was. I knew mine, right off the bat: my future husband.

That was my Isaac.

Next, Dad asked us to all find someone to pray with. To share our "Isaac" and pray for one another, giving it to the Lord, wholeheartedly.

A silver haired lady named Margaret came and sat down by me. She had kind brown eyes and a smile that could light up a room. I told her all about my "Isaac." How at just seventeen, my dream in life was to get married. I'd given my future man to the Lord several years ago and wore this purity ring to remind me to wait for and pray for "him." But, I was struggling. I wanted "him" now! And I felt very strongly that the Lord was asking me to lay "him" down. To trust. To surrender. And to be still and know: He is God.

Margaret's eyes softened. She looked at me, a young girl fifty years her junior, and told me how she had done the same. How she'd prayed for her now-husband. And how he'd come along, at the perfect time. They served the Lord together now as pastors in Ireland.

She prayed for my man. She prayed for his protection. She prayed for my heart; that I would be strong and wait, and give him to the Lord. And, that I would be made into a woman of faith who would bless "him." She prayed that "he" would be a godly, good, holy

man and that the Lord would be the one who
miraculously brought us together.

At the perfect time.

Plow Your Fields and Build Your House

Daniel *breathed* music these days. His teacher, Dr. Zhu,
offered him and Caleb full-ride scholarships to the
University of Central Oklahoma. Wow. Yet, at this
same time, Terry left his long time career and decided
to start a construction business. Daniel and the older
boys spent time that year doing construction jobs with
church friends on the side, learning the trade, and
Daniel knew he wanted to help his dad start this
family business. He declined the scholarship.

Daniel learned much in those years. How to work
hard, very hard. How to lead and manage life and
business.

And during those years of working oh so hard, he
made a lot of money which he diligently saved.

He dreamed of having land of his own, someday. He
loved   Oklahoma and imagined and dreamed often
about what it would be like to save up enough money
to buy his own little plot of land, build his own little
house, and have his own little family and life there.

He often read Proverbs 24:27, "Put your outdoor
work in order and get your fields ready; after that,

build your house."

He desired to get his "fields" – his life – ready for marriage. Not doing stupid, wasteful things that teenagers do or spending all his money on frivolous things and his time on girls. He desired to be wise and invest in his future marriage.

So he worked and prayed, saved and dreamed.

The Hope Chest, Love Letters, and a Heartache

For my eighteenth birthday, Mom and Dad gave me a beautifully handcrafted hope chest made of real oak. Sturdy and heavy.

And a few large cream-colored Pottery Barn boxes tied up in light green ribbon.

I bought a lot of home things, wedding things, and baby things. Pink cutting boards. Wedding scrapbooks. A tiny pink dress for our first daughter. I could see our home and our family all lined in up a row. How beautiful it would be!

Someday, soon, obviously.

I worked as a music teacher two days a week and a secretary at dad's office three, filling in the rest of my time with high school algebra and Charles Dickens novels. Life seemed to be going wonderfully, and I was pocketing some money, to boot. Every pay check, I would sneak into the nearest Pottery Barn and head right over to their dishware section. Every two weeks, I'd purchase a gravy boat here, a dinner plate there and carefully stash it away in my big oak chest, with a prayer and a kiss.

Years earlier, in a craft store, I'd found a special box, pale yellow and covered in a wildflower print. Mandy and I had seen the movie "Kate and Leopold" when it released, and I became enamored with the character of Leopold. A true, respectful gentleman. And so I began to fill my box with hand-written letters for my future husband. My "Leopold." At eighteen, it was more than half-full; I'd deemed it my "future husband letter box" at the age of fourteen.

Every Valentine's Day, instead of going on a date or hanging out with a boy I liked, I would sit down on my quilted bedspread and write a handwritten love letter to a man I'd not yet met or even seen.

"Darling,

I am thinking about you today and longing to know who you are…. I am praying for you. Wait for me, too."

"My sweet future man,

I am in Greece. On the beach, watching the sunset. Thinking of you. Here is a sea shell I picked up from the island of Mykonos. Darling, wait for me as I wait for you.

Your girl,

Erin"

A box for him, full of love. Full of hope. Full of faithfulness and prayers.

It helped me keep my focus on the Lord. It reminded me to pray for "him" and it helped me remember how important faithfulness was to me. In marriage, as well as *before* marriage. I dreamed of giving my husband that box on our wedding night, someday.

That fall, our family chose to leave our church. After ten years, it was time to move on, mostly because of the discord happening behind the scenes. Working as Dad's assistant at the church office, I often heard the head pastor yelling. We had to get out of there. Dad and I saw it, clearly every day.

What followed was brutally painful. People we considered real-life family, people we shared years of history with, people I led worship alongside and shared some of the most precious moments of my life with — people I trusted – turned their faces as our father and family were accused and slandered. All the while, behind their closed doors, they handled sacred things inappropriately. And we knew it.

It aches when people you've poured your heart into, prayed for, looked up to, and taken time to sit with and look in the eye and really know, and really love —

every single Sunday for years and years — treat you like a dirty, evil stranger.

People underestimate church splits. It's a huge loss. Like a kind of death. Uniquely searing, because God and faith and a lot of very messy, tender stuff is involved. Especially when you were as involved as my family. It was our life's blood, the thread that wove us together. It meant the world to us. Those weeks and months shook us. They rattled our family's hearts to our very core. I didn't understand it at all. I'd cry tears into my pillow at night. The kind that are big and hot and sting as they stick your hair to your cheeks. Crouched under my down comforter, in the fetal position, crying and crying until my abs ached like I'd done hundreds of sit-ups.

In my still-childlike heart and faith, I didn't understand how people who seemed so kind and good, who claimed the name of Jesus, could act so heartlessly. So cold. Certainly not like the Jesus *I knew*. I kept telling Mom, "But, as Christians, even if someone we love does something truly *awful*, shouldn't we … still love them? Pray for them? Forgive them? Care for them? Get them help? And we have done nothing wrong. I just don't understand how they could be so heartless." It literally boggled my mind and filled my eyes with tears that just wouldn't stop, for days on end. I couldn't piece it together. It was just so awful, and it hurt in places I didn't know were in my sensitive, never before hurt heart.

It was a defining moment for me. The first real hurt in life I'd ever experienced that a Band-Aid couldn't heal.

I had a choice to make: I could choose to lump these broken people together with my God and be angry and bitter, hurt and reeling. I could throw Him out with them, baby with the bathwater, and never believe or trust Him again. Or, I could carefully separate them. I could see the difference: their hot mess sin in shambles, hurting and stabbing my family. And Him, above and separated. Good, kind, sovereign and holy. Desperately sad for how His babies hurt each other so heartlessly, I would pray and pray, pressing into Him deeply. And for that, I wouldn't change a thing.

One night that winter as I wept and writhed on my bed alone at night in the dark, I noticed a full and shining moon pouring light through my white curtained window. And I swear, I saw a vision of Jesus. He sat at the foot of my black iron bed, his knees curled to His chest, His head buried in His knees, His body shaking as He wept softly. Right along with me.

People sometimes roll their eyes at me and laugh, calling me a Jesus freak and say, "Hey, you don't know what those so-called Christians did to me. They screwed me over and you know what? I can't trust God now."

Don't tell me I don't know. Because I do.

Maybe they didn't really know Him, after all. Maybe He weeps and weeps over how they've treated you, His baby.

Time healed the wound, slowly, but left a scar. A scar I am now, in some ways, grateful for. Because it pushed me that much closer to Him. Even though, the betrayal still stings.

And probably always will.

Dad often took me outside on nights when the moon was full above the oak trees. He would put his arm around me and whisper, "The word of the Lord is true. The word of the Lord is true." It was our beacon of hope, the full moon. And our phrase of victory. I will never cease to be grateful for a father who trusted the Lord in loss like that.

Sadly, Justin, the young man my little heart was set on marrying…he disowned us, too. And it hurt. Looking back, it seems silly how attached I became to someone I didn't know all that well. It was a young girl's hopes and dreams, tied like a balloon on a string to a man she admired. I just felt sure he would be "the one." Losing him – as our family's friend – and my dreamed of future husband, stung. He came to our home one summer Sunday afternoon and said goodbye. He knew things were falling apart at the church and he announced to us that day, out of left field, that he was moving to the Midwest to be a pastor at a church who offered him a job.

Little did I know, my worst fear at that time would come true …. He was not "the one" and that was the last time I would ever see or speak with him.

A year went by and no word from Justin or any of our former friends at church. Desperate prayers, anger and disappointment welled up in my soul. The kind that makes you wild eyed and crazy and sad. The kind that keeps you crying and mourning at night, and going through the motions during the day. I began to realize my adoration and desire for him was more than just that he was godly or handsome or kind hearted — it was because he represented something greater, something huge to me — my history, my past, my story, and most importantly — my future, my future husband, and God's promises.

And, quite honestly, *my plan.*

My plans were well-laid out, very well thought-through, and quite perfect — if I do say so myself. They were full to the brim of fun and things falling right into place, just as I would like. People would act as I would want them to, and I would be the center and the queen. I wouldn't need to learn anything, at all. There would be no uncertainty, no struggles, no sickness, no sad tears, no disappointments, and certainly no loneliness.

Most importantly, you might notice, they required absolutely no waiting, whatsoever. But as we know with our yearly Thanksgiving meals and God-written stories: good, quality things of worth take time. And require some patience and waiting, learning and humbling, sacrifice and perhaps most importantly, faith.

I realized that in order to survive and not go certifiably insane, I must open my very-clenched hands and trust my all-knowing, all-wise God.

But, man, it was the hardest thing I had ever done.

In order to do that, I felt I just had to destroy the "things" I was holding onto that were reminders of him. The notes he had sent. The cards. All the sermons he'd preached at our church. And the sermons his father had preached in the eighties and nineties. I listened to them every night, and loved them with my whole heart. But, I had to cut ties and move on. Let it go. Let my plan go, and even – let my dreams go.

For His bigger, better ones. Dreams I could not even imagine or comprehend in my very much still-little girl Erin heart and mind at that season of my life.

Our house is set on the back side of a pine covered mountain in the Los Angeles National Forest, in a grove of old, large oak trees. That autumn afternoon, Mom, Dad, and Mandy left to run errands. I stayed back purposefully; knowing full well what I had to do.

Under my bed, I kept a big square shoebox. It was full

of his father's sermon tapes, the precious ones he preached at the Ranch and the baby church, before he died of cancer — his cards, photos of our sailing trip and things my family did with him. As the family shut the front door and I heard the car driving down the gravel driveway, I didn't even blink or think twice. Holding the box, I stood, looking out my large bright open window at the gigantic and two-hundred-year old oak tree I often stared out at as I dreamed, prayed and journaled in my room. I marched right downstairs, out the side door, and under the tree's long, arm-like branches that reached down, almost as if to hug you, with its green leaves frolicking above like confetti. In a strange, desperate, passionate fury, I grabbed dad's old shovel that leaned up against the green wall of the house, and I began digging a hole in the dusty, dry dirt — moving the oak tree leaves that had fallen and scooping up the brown sand-like soil. At the base of the large tree trunk — probably three feet by three feet — I dug, wild-eyed. As I thought about the last few months, I became angrier and angrier — not at Josh or the church people or my family — but at God. I can still so clearly remember that feeling, the first time things didn't really go according to my tightly held-onto plans. That feeling of "how could you let this happen? I thought You said You *loved* me? And now this?! You say You are good, but… how could any of this be good?" The first time — as a young, new adult — I had no choice but to let the chips fall where they may, say goodbye to people I loved, endure stinging betrayal and spine-chilling stabs in the back, and let go of my long-held, very beloved – and maybe, to the onlooker, a rather silly girlhood dream – but a dream, nevertheless.

Relationships, history, and future hopes; all crushed.

And life, as I knew it, changed forever.

I am, by nature, a deep feeler, and cannot help but let my feelings out. My plan for the special sentimental keepsakes and pieces of the story and history was to bury them under the dirt. To carefully, gently, and tenderly lay the once-treasured (and really, still-treasured) items and sermon tapes into a shallow grave. To "say goodbye" to the dream and leave it in the past, to grieve over it softly and slowly, and maybe cry a little. Like a beloved pet, covering it up carefully and maybe even planting a flower bush over it, watering it with my tears, and then walking away quietly; perhaps a picture of "moving on." If you cannot already gather, I was *extremely* mellowdramatic.

But the planned sacred moment turned out to be very different than I imagined. I was not slow or gentle. I wasn't loving or careful, but rather wild eyed and quick. Certainly, this was not my shining moment. Or my proudest. It is one I regret, more than anything. But, in that moment, I needed a physical picture of surrender.

Wielding the shovel in one hand, I grabbed the box and laid it into the dirt hole. I began digging again, lifting up piles of dirt and throwing them on the items. Furiously and hard. And out there, in the middle of the mountains, on those twenty-eight acres, alone — I began to talk to the Lord. Out loud. Telling Him everything.

Scoop. Lift. Pour. Dropping dirt onto the box.

"Why???" I began, as if I was arguing with a brother.

"Like, seriously?! Why did you take them all away from us? I thought 'he' was the one. My heart *knew*."

"Lord….. Lord?!"

Scoop, lift, pour.

"My heart is broken! How could you let this happen! No. No no no, Lord! Please! How dare you!!!!"

And I rammed the shovel into the tapes and paper, crushing them, mangling them, destroying every last one — as hard as my little arms could hit with that heavy steel shovel head. Until the plastic went flying and the tapes were shredded and scattered in long strings and short blunt cuts.

It was not a pretty scene. It was a struggle. It was very honest and raw. And if an onlooker heard it, they probably would have been quite offended, and thought I was a little crazy.

But, it was real. All my thoughts and feelings poured

out in words, to Him who knows and sees and hears all anyway. For the very first time, in response to grief and loss, I gave it to Him.

My hands shook hard and slow as I stood there, holding the shovel. It felt very heavy. Tears fell from my eyes and I wept, deeply and loudly, thankful my family was gone for the day. Weeping turned into wailing, echoing through the trees, down the canyon, up the mountain. I wept until I fell to the ground, still holding the standing shovel. I sat on the now-covered hole full of my broken (and now, mangled) dream and bitter disappointment.

"Lord, I do not understand your ways….. I hate this plan…. But I trust You."

Sobs shook my thin frame as I laid in the dirt and whispered,

"You are good. You are good. I love you. You are good. I worship you. I worship you ….You are good. I trust you. I worship you."

I left the hurt there. At the foot of the cross. I opened my hands and gave it all to Him. That was the day I left it, buried it, and moved on. In the future, I would feel sad about the things that happened — sometimes, I still feel that sting when I think through the friendships lost in that church split, the way my little girl heart ached so innocently and fearfully. But, I truly did leave it to Him. And when I gave it to Him, feeling it all and not pretending one bit, I was free.

That evening, as the sun set and the full moon rose, Dad motioned for me to come outside with him. Overcome with the weariness and emotion of the past few months, I slipped under his big arm and looked out, over the oak grove up into the navy blue sky, stars coming out twinkling. A big golden moon stood perfectly full and round as can be, shining bright and purposefully.

Unwavering.

Dad told me, "Someday, you will tell this story – all you are going through now – and lots and lots of young women's lives are going to be changed."

"Yeah right." I whimpered. But I hoped and prayed he was right. (Oh, how he was!)

That day, I left my heartache under that tree. Mangled and messy, ugly, angry and hurt.

Little did I know then, that *exactly* ten years later, I would stand again under that same oak tree, right over that shallow grave, in a white lace dress, across from my beaming, beautiful man. On my wedding day. And say my vows.

But He knew. And I believe, as surely as He wept with His little girl then, He also smiled. Because He could see it all, and had already begun to weave a beautiful story and plan out of the brokenness, redeeming all the tears and fury.

The word of the Lord is true.

The Horrible Goodbye

A thirteenth child joined the Morris family! Little Mercy. The eleventh, Joel spent three perfectly healthy years playing on the farm with his siblings. Outgoing, friendly, funny, and very smart for his age. He and his twin, Josiah, celebrated their third birthday in September of 2006. On the first of October, Joel began running mysterious fevers. After a few rounds of fevers, Terry and Cindy took him to a doctor and were told his iron was low. For the next few weeks, they tested his blood twice a week. On December fourth, the doctor examined bumps on Joel's little head – which they found out were tumors. Joel was admitted to the hospital and went through extensive testing.

The horrible diagnosis confirmed: Joel was at stage IV (the most advanced stage) of Neuroblastoma.

A childhood cancer.

The Morris family began to pray, intercede, and beg the Lord to heal their son, hoping and praying God would use chemotherapy treatments to heal Joel's body.

After eight and a half days in the hospital, Joel was able to spend Christmas at home, with his family.

He then returned to the hospital for another round of chemo.

It was painful beyond words and more overwhelming than his family could bear. They took him to the Lord in prayer, all day and all night. It was frightening and dreadful.

During an agonizing bone marrow test, Joel asked for Daniel, over and over again. "Dos...Dos..." (his nickname for his beloved older brother.)

After the test, Daniel held Joel close, for hours.

On January 3rd, 2007, at midnight, Joel went into a coma. He experienced a seizure. A tumor began to bleed in his head and caused his brain to swell.

After undergoing testing, Joel's doctor declared him "brain dead." He insisted Joel be taken off life support. The Morris family did not agree with his definition of "death." They stood on the scripture that says "life is in the blood." And until Joel's heart stopped beating on its own – naturally – he was very much alive.

In a terribly painful turn of events, the doctor took the Morris family to court in order to force them to take Joel off life support. During that time the family cared for Joel, in the hospital. His parents learned how to care for him when the nurses refused.

The family began to prepare to bring Joel home.

On January 23rd, 2007, Joel's heart stopped beating.

As his mama wrote: "He went to be with the Lord Jesus, in heaven. Our lives are changed forever. God is faithful in the midst of this trial and we look with great hope to be with him someday."

During Joel's illness, a Christian filmmaker took footage and when Joel passed away, he interviewed the Morris family. He created a DVD documentary called *Joel's Journey*, to tell his story and to point to the value of life and fighting for it. Daniel and Caleb created a beautiful music score for the film. Joel's story touched (and continues to touch) thousands of lives.

The shadow of sorrow hung over the Morris family. They missed Joel so much, and life would never be the same without him. They mourned and grieved.

Daniel continued to work hard, saving all his pennies for his dreamed of land. His friend, Dave, encouraged the twins to save, save, save. And not spend. "You can do it, you can make it happen if you want to. You can get that land." Working long, hot days building outdoors, Daniel and Caleb often enjoyed cold cokes as a small refreshment. Dave figured out that one can of coke equaled four square feet of Oklahoma land

and he encouraged the twins to forgo the pleasure –
they would be one step closer to that dreamed of
property.

Soon, Daniel and Caleb found the perfect pieces of
land. It was a long, six-month process of finding
records, closing, and paperwork.

Finally, after years of dreaming, working, and saving
hard- earned cash, Daniel and his best friend twin
owned their very own pieces of Oklahoma.
They each owned twenty beautiful acres, side by side.

They celebrated like crazy! They now had their own
land to work and trees to cut down! It was amazing!

It was a very impressive and well-earned
accomplishment for young men of twenty-two.

The twins set to working on their land, every
weekend. Every spare moment.

Drawing up plans for his home, by hand, Daniel
dreamed up a lovely log cabin. He drew out and
imagined the rooms, the big fireplace, the nooks and
crannies.

He also noticed the daughter of a family friend that
year. She was sweet and pretty. During this time,
Caleb met a sassy young woman from the East Coast
and began a romance of his own. Daniel tried to

pursue his love interested, but soon realized it wasn't right.

He continued to wait and pray for "his girl." He was happy for Caleb, though it was a new season when the twins, for the first time ever, were not always together, side by side. Soon, Caleb moved to Maryland to be closer to his new girlfriend, while Daniel stayed home. Change was in the air.

Psalm 84:11

I applied for a singular college. "My plan" did not include attending college, sadly. I had planned to get married and start a big family *as soon as possible* after turning eighteen. But (thankfully) the Lord's ideas for my life were far and beyond anything I dreamed up.

Hidden in a tree-covered canyon near LA, it was a conservative, Christian college with one major that piqued my interested: Home Economics, Family and Consumer Sciences. My ultimate dream: to be a wife, mother, homemaker, to run my own home business, to write and to minister to women. These things were all the focus of the major. It seemed like the perfect fit.

I spent my first year commuting because I lived one hour away, off campus, at our home on the mountain. It proved to be a smooth way to transition from homeschool to college life.

Second year, I moved into the dorms. And life

changed.

I still remember exactly what the all-girls dormitory, nestled in the line of tall, old pine trees, smelled like. Old and musty. The stairs were creaky and white. My new home: Dixon, Room 111.

Let's face it: Dixon was known as the "not-cool" girl's dorm. The (precious and godly) girls who typically lived in Dixon were not known — as a group — as the athletic ones, the preppy ones, or the popular ones. The girls in Dixon were known throughout our fairly tiny college campus as slightly dorky, always wearing dresses and long jean skirts, and there was a stereotype that us Dixon girls were "Home Ec" majors. Which was partly true. I lived there, and many of my classmates did as well.

That first year was a little tough.

Because I was *not* one of the cool girls. Later, in my last year of college on that same campus, I blossomed. I learned how to fit in. I learned how to be like everybody else, get people to like me, and for better or for worse, be popular. I would build friendships – some real, some fake. Later, I would become a Resident Assistant (a leader in charge of a wing of twenty-five young women) in the "coolest" dorm on campus: the dorm full of athletes.

But, that first year? I felt dorky and very much alone.

I was a formerly homeschooled girl, with pretty bad fashion sense — well, good fashion sense in theory. I poured over *InStyle* and *Vogue* magazine every month and studied photos of Katie Holmes and Victoria Beckham at New York Fashion Week. But I wore what I could afford. It's pretty hard to be fashionable when your wallet is empty.

I was timid and afraid.

And honestly? A little skittish and shy around all the well-honed students who knew and "got" this school drill, the ones who seemed to flit around confidently, smiling and waving and batting their eyelashes at everyone as if they knew them. I didn't know a soul.

I remember sitting at my dorm window, watching the rain drops fall on the glass one of my first nights living on campus. I'd never lived anywhere but at home with Mom, Dad, and Mandy before. This experience was new, and scary.

The popular, pretty girls who wore designer jeans and drove fancy cars, would often whisk off to a night of fun at a concert in the city. They always invited my roommate — a good hearted, energetic, former cheerleader with the prettiest dark curls and a heart for God. She was sweet and we were fast friends. But those popular girls never invited me. It made me feel small and silly, left out and awkward. It made my nose feel wider and my hair frizzier. I'd never felt that way, before. Not on the Ranch or at the church. I always felt accepted, looked up to, and admired, even. It was a new day. A humbling day.

I was a nobody out in this big new world.

And not one boy noticed me. "Man," I thought.

"This is gonna be harder (and scarier) than I realized…"

All the popular, rich, pretty girls got up early, curled their hair and applied their Chanel makeup. They got coffee for each other from Starbucks, and saved seats for each other at Chapel. They wore J. Crew headbands and necklaces, Seven Jeans, Louis Vuitton bags. They always saved my roommate a seat, in the front row.

I always wandered into Chapel late.

College was so new, and I was tired, not used to the rigorous schedule of Chapel three times a week, night class, morning class, and afternoon class. Church on Sunday, new friends, dorm life, and dorm events. Sharing a tiny room with a practical stranger. Homework. Oh so much homework. I absolutely dreaded the mornings because I had no one to sit by at Chapel. I always slid into the back row or maybe a random bleacher near the foreign exchange students.

I remember feeling so alone, like I didn't belong anywhere in this big new world.

I would sweat as Chapel wore on, wondering who I would sit by at lunch at the cafeteria…. would I sit alone? Maybe I could just take my food to go and eat it in the bathroom? My room? *"I'll take it "to go" in one of those white Styrofoam boxes and grab a couple white plastic forks and eat at my dorm room's desk, pretending to have homework to do. I hate Styrofoam."*

I'd figure it out.

My heart would pound while the popular girls flirted with boys and fluttered around the room so easily. Why was it so hard for me?

It was like that those first few semesters. Like some sort of smaller, sad Christian version of *Mean Girls*. A few girls in particular always teased me and made condescending comments about my clothes or my strawberry blonde hair. It made me feel about one inch tall.

I was *desperate*. Desperate for a boy, any boy, to like me. But no one gave me a passing glance. No one. Not a soccer player or baseball player. Not a theology student or a pastor in training.

If only I had known… a boy out in a field in rural Oklahoma was not drinking Cokes to save for land he had his eye on. For us, someday.

If only I had known then.

I would have been much more contented. If only.

Honestly, I became obsessed with finding a husband. That's the truth of it, spelled out and not all that pretty. I wanted to get married, passionately, from the age of about sixteen. So by twenty? I was hot on the chase.

Yes, I gave God the "pen" to write my love story, years before. Trusting in His sovereign, good plan -- eager to look to Him, wait on Him, and worship Him in my waiting. Knowing that His pick of a husband for me would be far and above any love story I could muster up. Yet, I struggled with it. It wasn't an easy thing for me.

I was sick of the pattern: I would find the perfect husband candidate and then the Lord would sit me down and say, "No, no, Darling. Not yet." I wrestled with the Lord weekly. Some days, I trotted around independent and confident, just *sure* "my man" would be coming along at the perfect time. Other days I basked in my close and "just us" relationship with the Love of My Life, Jesus. And other days, I dragged myself out of my dorm bed, moaning and whining to God inwardly as I watched happy couples twittering past, rolling my eyes and asking, "Ummm, where is 'he'? And why the heck is this taking so long, Lord? Can't you see I'm ready? Really? Another Thanksgiving and Christmas alone? I can't do this." Which was followed by some whining, crying, singing along to sad love songs, and then giving it to Him again. Truly. But often with a disappointed little heart.

The struggle was real.

Whether I would really admit it or not, having a boyfriend, being pursued by a great guy, and being married were this elusive thing: the key to unlock perfection in my life, the magic spell that would make everything better, the sprinkle of fairy dust that would make life just that much more sparkly. The sunshine on dark days.

I held that little idol up, high and shining, determined to find my man, and desperate to make something happen.

When really, I just needed Jesus.

Coffee dates with a few guys. Crushes on a few more. I tried to push-through dating a young man I met that first semester. He looked nice and had a pretty perfect face. Soon, I found out, he was crazy as a loon. Yet, I ignored that for a while…hoping *something* might work out. Thankfully, that one didn't.

My roommate and I prayed, fervently, every night, for our future husbands. I was blessed to share a room with a kindred spirit who also loved and waited for her future "man."

Psalm 84:11 became our anthem. We recited it, read it, memorized it, reminded each other of it, wrote it on napkins and index cards and in texts to each other on our cool gray flip phones. We'd like boys on campus. They wouldn't work out. We'd cry hot tears on our small dorm beds, opening our hands to Jesus, surrendering through clenched teeth. Then trusting Him, again.

"For the Lord God is a sun and shield; the Lord bestows favor and honor. No good thing does He withhold from those who walk uprightly."
Psalm 84:11

"So, if it is not good for me right now, then He won't give it. Right?"

Right.

"Because, if it was good for me today, He would give it to me."

That's right.

We reminded each other, daily.

If you found your way down those white stairs to Dixon 111 today, I'm very sure you could still hear our nightly prayers, echoing in those halls. (I'm very sure you'd hear some belly laughter, too. Hilarious times were had with our wing mates in our cozy room that year.)

As college continued, singleness seemed to be the

name of my game. I felt left out and lonely most of the time. Yet, my standards were high for what I desired in a husband. And even in a campus of one thousand students who loved Jesus? I couldn't see my future husband. Anywhere.

One evening during my fall semester, Dad invited me to a meeting with some of his pastor friends, including Jack Hayford. He felt I'd be encouraged. I sat at the back wall with Dad. Dick Mills spoke on stage, an elderly man with a lifetime of ministry behind him. During the end of his talk, while worship music played softly, he shared words from the Lord with various people in the room. He'd give them a scripture the Lord put on his heart for them, and a specific word of encouragement to go along with it. At the close of the evening, he pointed to me. I didn't expect it.

He said: "He that believeth shall not make haste. God will open doors in your life that no one can shut and He will shut doors that no one will open. Cool it, kid."

He read Isaiah 45:2-3, *"I will go before you and level the exalted places, I will break in pieces the doors of bronze and cut through the bars of iron, I will give you the treasures of darkness and the hoards in secret places, that you may know that it is I, the Lord, the God of Israel, who calls you by your name."*

And Isaiah 30:21: *"And your ears shall hear a word behind you saying, 'This is the way, walk in it.' When you turn to the right or when you turn to the left."*

Pretty clear, Lord.

Those words strengthened me to go on. Even though, in all honesty, I didn't *love* them when I first heard them. I wanted what I wanted, *now*! But His plans were better than mine. And at the end of the day, I trusted Him. Those words Dick Mills told me were scribbled on a piece of paper he later gave me.

It is still in my Bible, today.

The Land Down Under

After dating for four months, Daniel broke up with his first girlfriend. A wholesome girl in Bible school, they would talk and hold hands. They were friends, but there really wasn't a spark.

He wanted a change. To get out of town. His feet ached for travel, and he wanted to see the world. Like a cat in a cage, he was ready to get out and have some adventures.

Randomly, he emailed the organization of YWAM in Townsville, Australia. He offered to volunteer and serve. With his construction and music skills, could they use some helping hands?

They replied, immediately.

He raised $9,000 for his missions work and hopped on a plane.

In January he left the freezing cold Oklahoma ground and stepped into that tropical, lush, and humid paradise.

He lived on base, doing lots of construction and working to repair a medical ship YWAM sent to Papua, New Guinea, for mission work. Playing worship with the band in off-time, he realized afresh how much he loved music.

The day after he arrived, one of the leaders approached Daniel. He looked him square in the eye and asked, "What lights a fire in your soul?"

"Music."

Why am I not pursuing music more? He wondered. He began to play again, often and passionately.

On the weekends, he travelled all around. He sailed to the islands, visited one of the top ten most beautiful beaches in the world, and went scuba diving in the Great Barrier Reef. Those days were full of new and exciting adventures.

The YWAM girls had their eyes on Daniel. In fact, they went crazy over him. A southern gentleman who loved Jesus, had tan washboard abs, and played the violin beautifully? They chased him and fought over him. He had his eye on a girl in Maryland. It wouldn't work out with her in the end, but (lucky for me) his affection for her in that time kept him from pursuing any of the girls in Australia, flocking around him like flies to honey.

Fast Cars and Freedom

He was from a tiny town somewhere in Kansas. I'd never known anyone from the Midwest before. We met in a nighttime astronomy class. His name was Tyler. We started chatting and hanging out in the lounge, and I thought he was cute. Dark blonde hair and dark brown eyes. Maybe a wee bit immature... but, cute. Not exactly what I was planning... but, nice.

And the way he looked at me.... *Finally*: I needed it.

I was tired of waiting. Of being the single one. I was so freaking sick of sitting in class and chapel alone. Sick of being the only girl who didn't have a built-in date for Spring Party. Weary of being the one who never had a boyfriend. Who went on one-time coffee dates, and was the gal pal. I wanted to be wanted and like and loved. I could almost *hear* the clock ticking. Three months.... three months Erin.... and then you will be *done with college*. You will have to find a real job and provide for yourself. You will be walking onto that stage, receiving your diploma from Dr. John MacArthur and venturing out into the real and very scary world. *Alone*.

It haunted me like a ghost at night and hung around me like a stalker during the day.

I was crazy for love, desperate for companionship. I needed my man. I needed "him." I was ready to be the girlfriend, the pursued one, the wanted one. The bride, the wife, the mama. Why not me? Why? I would cry at night. And now, a Hollister-wearing boy with a Midwestern twang and big muscles was looking at me *like that*.

The way he talked to me? And followed me around?

Stick a fork in me, I was done.

He wore bright pink t-shirts. He was more cocky than confident.

We quickly became official boyfriend and girlfriend.

I graduated, one class shy of a diploma.

And then, he went home for the summer.

Between school semesters, he worked as a roofer in Kansas City. He'd call me at night and we'd talk, for an hour or so.

It felt nice being wanted, but there wasn't a spark. I couldn't deny it. It bothered me and hung over my head.

He never bought me flowers.

We spent the summer apart, talking on the phone.

And then, he returned to California.

Soon after, I knew, beyond a shadow of a doubt, that he was not my future husband. I'd been denying it for a while because, well, it was nice to have "someone." He wasn't a bad guy, but he was not mine. Not my kindred spirit.

Eight months of dating, and I didn't love him. I liked him and I liked not being alone, but I knew he did not make my heart skip a beat the way it should. He didn't really give me butterflies. He wasn't the man I'd been praying for…for the past nine years of my life.

One evening, as he hung out with me at my new apartment, Mandy and her boyfriend in the next room, we lounged on the floor (we had no furniture and no budget for furniture at the time.) As I wrapped a birthday present for one of my best friends, we talked.

Eight months of dating, and we'd never kissed.

In fact, I had never kissed anyone.

Years ago, when I decided to save myself — my heart, mind, and body for my future husband, I gave God all my kisses….and, everything else. That kind of commitment is certainly not on everyone's heart, and it's not everyone's story. For some, it's right to kiss before you meet your man. But it was the path I had chosen and it was important to my heart.

Kissing became something I held very sacredly in my hands. I once heard a pastor at the Ranch explain that "to worship" the Lord in the original Greek meant "to kiss." Kissing. Like my sacred, special worship of the Lord? A picture of that with my husband?

Sacred and special, indeed.

Guarding it, purposefully saving it, for my man.

My dream was to kiss my husband, only.

I prayed it would be so.

In that moment in my apartment, my boyfriend asked if he could kiss me. It was not really a romantic moment, at all. I, sick with a horrible cold. He, sprawled out on my dingy brown carpet. It wasn't really crazy at all for him to think it normal to kiss his girlfriend after eight months of dating. But, somehow, in that moment…. I *just could not.* I can hardly explain it. My girlfriends later begged me, "What?! Why didn't you just kiss the guy! Come on!" But I couldn't. I literally couldn't. I don't think there would've been anything necessarily wrong with kissing him. It just did not feel right.

Now, I know, the Lord's hand was on me that night. Answering my prayers, making future dreams come true.

Like a wall between us, in that moment. I sat straight up and said, "No…I am so sorry. But, no. I just can't."

Clear as day, I can recall in my mind the moment I knew, for sure, he was not my husband.

One hot august afternoon my grandma Dot and her best friend Sharon (who is a second grandmother to me) stopped by my new apartment, sweetly making a trip across town to see it. Mandy and I moved into our own place, for the first time ever. Our apartment was grimy, in a dangerous part of town, and completely overpriced. Every night, at one in the morning, I heard digging outside in the dark, hidden alley beneath my bedroom window. The place was pretty rough and rent was high; more than $1,000 per month. But we were proud to have our own place. Dot helped us get it, and it was very important to share it with her. It meant a lot to me.

That day, I knew full well: He was not the man for me.

Because, really? He was just a boy.

The apartment was on the second floor of the building and a long, steep flight of stairs led up to our front door. Sharon, recovering from knee surgery, needed a hand up the stairs. The ladies are grandmothers. Offering them your arm? It was the obvious, polite, and gentlemanly thing to do.

I had to *ask* him to notice.

And then? He *rolled his eyes* when I motioned to him, whispering and asking him to help my grandmothers up the stairs.

My jaw fell to the floor when he begrudgingly did it, with a sigh.

I realized he didn't really care about me. That he would not have the capacity or character to honor me as the years wore on.

I could see it, right then and there. I could see us down the road. Married. I could see myself — pregnant. Unable to walk up the stairs in our apartment… would he scoff and roll his eyes then?

When I was 85 and crouched over and my boobs sagged and my hair was all gray and coarse?

When I was no longer "fun" or "hot" like I was now at age twenty-three?

If he wouldn't help my grandmas up a flight of stairs, if he didn't have the energy, care, patience, and kindness *now*, when he is trying to *win my heart*? Would he then?

When we have a screaming toddler and a hungry newborn and a whining puppy?

No. It was a bad sign. An omen I could see with my eyes — that my hunches were true, that my feelings were real....

He was not the one.

It came over me.

With a wave of nausea.

Oh, it hurt.

The next few days were a blur.

I flew to Arkansas, on a whim to visit a college friend. To clear my head. Little did I know, I flew into the town where my future husband was born. On the way back to her home, we took a wrong road and got lost in Oklahoma.

For a few days, I ate real Southern queso dip, watched Razorback games, and sipped Pumpkin Spice Lattes in a place that really felt like fall.

He texted me twice.

One text was something cold and weird.

Another? A photo of him on a hiking trip with some guy friend and the guy's uncommonly pretty sister. Several photos of my boyfriend and that girl popped up on Facebook. Huh.

I knew it. It was over. And I didn't even want him.

Jerk.

Landing at LAX, he refused to pick me up from the airport, even though he wasn't busy.

I demanded he come over to my apartment to talk. I was done with a capital D.

Half my heart threw up my arms and yelled: "No time for losers!"

The other half wept

Oh… my heart.

I broke up with him.

I grieved like Marianne for Willoughby. I was so distraught that I became ill. I laid on the dingy, ratty orange-brown carpet of my apartment (because, Mandy and I still couldn't afford beds or couches; heck, we could barely afford food…and parting with *four* quarters to wash a load of laundry was simply too much) for two straight days. Rich, creamy, spicy, sugary Chai Tea Lattes from Starbucks — the only "food" I could bear passing my lips.

Stricken with sorrow, I could hardly move. My friends and family began to wonder, actually, and gingerly, yet confusedly ask, "I though *you* broke up with *him?* You swore you didn't want this. Remember?"

I remembered. I did not want *this*, but I wanted "it." I wanted my "him." And the reality of *I am twenty-three and completely and utterly single* began to set in.

Hard.

Looking back now, a few years later, twenty-three is *oh so young*, and I was (and am, in general) oh so dramatic!

 But, hearts break, for different reasons in different seasons.

For me, back then, in the place I was: it was searing heart ache.

Those days rolled on like a lonely, ugly blur.

I would roll out of bed at 7:55am, brush my teeth and wash my face. I never bothered to put make up on anymore. My trusty black hair ties were my only beauty "help." I'd twist my hair into a wild top knot, and pour a cup of bitter and sweet coffee — sometimes, if I had my shiz together enough. I'd tear to work in my breaking down ugly green Honda

Taurus, blasting sad country songs all the way on my fuzzy radio.

When night came, it all hit like a Mack truck.

One late evening, I crept out to the fridge.

Mandy's boyfriend had brought over one of those big glass jugs of cheap sangria and it was chilling in the fridge door. You know, the ones that cost three dollars and taste exactly like sugary rubbing alcohol. I slipped into the kitchen at 1:00 AM, found a cracked green plastic margarita glass in our rotted wooden cupboard and poured myself a *very* large glass.

All I'd eaten that day was a Grande Pumpkin Spice Latte with soy milk and an 8-count Chick Fil A nugget box with some buffalo sauce, no fries. When I'm happy, I am hungry as a horse. When I'm sad, my appetite is the size of a hamster's.

I sat up in bed, all alone. The shoveling, again. What the heck was that? Whatever it was, it was freaking hair-raising and more than a little foreboding. And the neighbor who lived beneath me? I could hear her snoring, loud and clear, every night from around midnight until it was time to go to work.

This was *so* not how life was supposed to turn out. I rolled my eyes and wiped a tear from my cheek. This was so far from the dream. I mean, pretty much as far as you could get. Post-college and a failed graduate?

Single with absolutely no man who desired me to speak of? A nanny? Really? After all my ministry and plans and dreams and music and writing….

I was changing the diapers and folding the underwear that belonged to the babies and husband of some other woman?

This was it, Lord? Really? Okay. Wow.

I felt bitter and angry and very, very much alone.

Ugh. *I can't do this, Lord.* What is your plan?! This is not how this was supposed to turn out… remember? Remember Your promises? All that stuff you said and all those prayers I prayed? Where are You?

I quickly sipped the bitter wine.

The room began to spin.

I'd never, ever, *ever* been drunk before. And in my twenty-three years of life, I'd probably enjoyed a total of three drinks you need an ID for.

So that wide, dollar store margarita glass full of cheap sangria combined with a completely empty stomach and absolutely zero tolerance of strong drinks did me in that night, and I passed out on my mattress on the brown ratty carpet.

An hour later, I woke up, heaving all over the bed.

The next morning, horrified and ashamed, I called the lady I babysat for.

"I'm sorry, I have a bad stomach ache… I can't come today."

She sounded like she thought I was lying.

My throat burned.

I laid back on my bed, holding tightly onto my thin, worn top sheet, the comforter and blanket now thrown into the laundry basket, all stained with red, of course.

I shut my eyes against the cruel world. This is not what I expected. Not at all.

The Depths of Despair

Driving, aimlessly. Through winding Maryland roads.

After three months in the land Down Under, Daniel moved to the East Coast – to meet the girl he had his eye on and to pursue music. Things didn't work out with the girl. She led him on, dragged him around, and broke his precious heart.

He went spiraling down a black hole.

With his heart heavy, and his mind fuzzy, Daniel stopped in the parking lot of a McDonald's. He didn't know where he was going or what he was doing.

Darkness just engulfed his heart and it was pressing in.

Whispering lies in his mind turned into yells, and yells turned into screams.

Lately, life had been hard. He'd been living in a new state, carving out work and chasing after the dream of being a professional viola player.

And, although he rejoiced with Caleb on his recent marriage and new baby on the way, he couldn't help but feel left alone.

Darkness began to engulf him.

He felt down and weary.

He felt as though he couldn't make any decisions.

He felt incompetent.

He couldn't remember how to play his viola, pick up tools and work construction.

His twin and sister-in-law bent down and reminded him how to tie his shoes. He simply couldn't remember.

He felt lost and alone. And overcome with fear.

Fearful of doing almost anything. He lost confidence.

He felt like he couldn't play music well, anymore.

Satan whispered lies to him.

"Nothing you do is good enough."

He couldn't take it.

Sometimes, he thought of ending his own life.

He spiraled into a depression, a deep, dark pit of depression, and he didn't think he could ever climb his way out of that black, ugly hole.

Sitting in his truck, he felt blank.

Back in Oklahoma, Elijah felt the Lord place it on his heart to call his brother. Right now. He picked up the phone and it rang. Daniel, sitting in the McDonald's parking lot, answered.

He asked how he was. He could tell Daniel was down. Lost.

And he began to speak truth.

He preached to his brother, over the phone line.

"Take the Lord's hand! He is there, just reach out and take his hand. He is light! He is hope! Man, you have to look to Him, and speak truth – these are *lies*. Take His hand!"

It was a ray of light, a lighthouse of hope in a very rocky, stormy, and dark sea.

The depression continued for three months. Three months of complete darkness.

So dark, his family worried they might lose him.

One Sunday morning, he walked into church. During the service, Daniel sat, lifeless. He didn't even want to be there.

At the end of his sermon, the preacher stopped for a moment. He shared that – in the room of 3,000 – the Lord told him there was someone dealing with depression and suicidal thoughts. He felt the Lord wanted the person to know there is freedom and hope. He will bring you through this. It will not last.

Daniel knew he was talking to him.

A few days later, Caleb took Daniel to meet with the pastor. He sat in the truck for two whole hours before he went in.

Lie upon lie screamed in his mind, lies from the enemy. He felt too proud, too scared, and he didn't know what he'd say.

Finally, he went into the pastor's office.

He told Daniel he'd been through the same battle with darkness and encouraged him to fight the lies with the Word of God and to focus on scripture; to recite it over and over and over again. And when the lies reared their ugly heads, to hit them down with scripture. Until they went away.

It began to work. Through constant encouragement from his family, he began to emerge from the thick darkness.

He went home to the farm to spend some time with the family. His little sisters explain how down he had become, how it scared them. How they'd cry, it was all so sad. He was like a shell of who he used to be, engulfed in sadness and lies.

His mom still cries when she talks about that dark, dark season. She says it felt like Joel's sickness. Like losing a child. Again.

Slowly but surely, the light broke through.

And the Lord healed him with His word. With His truth. Grace flowed down and covered him and God rescued him from the darkness. He shot down the lies of Satan, every time they popped up again, with the Word of God. Over and over, again and again.

He began to heal.

The Empire State Building

A failed attempt at moving out of my hometown. A failed attempt at three different jobs. A failed relationship. A failure at truly finishing college.

All the things I found my identity in: being a college student, a worship leader, a leader in the dorms, a youth leader at my church, a musician, a girlfriend, a Home Ec major. Stripped away from me. Who was I? What was I called to do?

Lord, did you forget all of Your promises?

I began to fall apart.

To this day, I truly believe I had some kind of emotional and mental breakdown that year. 2011. I flipped out. I left my job, my lease and apartment with a friend in Orange County. I moved home with Mom and Dad. I couldn't deal anymore. My breakdown was misunderstood by all my friends from college. They attacked and confronted me, when I really needed them to just sit beside me, hug me, and ask, "Hey, are you okay? Can I help you?" It hurt. It reminded me of the betrayal I went through after our church split, and then it hurt, all the more. It made me run.

Twenty-four and single. Moneyless. Jobless. Carless. Taking refuge back in my girlhood bedroom. No college diploma because I didn't finish one stupid class.

I'd hit rock bottom. For real.

Thank God for Mom and Dad's grace and faithful love.

It's hard watching your friends ride off into perfectly pink and yellow sunsets, kissing their dream husbands and rubbing big, round baby bumps. It's hard to see your expectations let down and your dreams fail. It's hard to be confused and lost. It's hard to try to make it at a new job and realize you're not a good fit.

The twenties can be hard. Leaving home can be hard. Leaving college can be hard. Breakups are hard. Going it alone as a single working girl in a rough economy is hard. Life is hard.

Living back on the mountain with Mom and Dad, I was grateful for a safety net to fall into. But I felt like a total failure.

Mom told me maybe this was a new beginning. Dad told me to write.

I got a nanny job. I played dolls with two toddler girls. I mopped their mom's kitchen floor. I folded their dad's shirts. I wept every night.

How did I end up doing all the things I dreamed of: caring for a home, raising babies.... for another woman? I was living my dream, but for someone else. It made me feel small, awful and disappointed.

I prayed like crazy those days and somehow I was led to start a blog.

I wrote, honestly, about my heart. My heart for Jesus and for waiting. I named my blog "Sweetness Itself." Because I wanted to hear His sweet whispers. I wanted to speak them to young women.

My broken and hurting heart welled up with a passionate desire to love on, speak to, write to, and be real with other women. To tell them about Him and to be in community with them. I began to make friends all over the world, through my blog. I wrote a few posts about waiting for my future husband, that went viral. I began to love writing and connecting.

Out of my brokenness, I began to find my ministry.

One crisp evening, I entered a giveaway on one of my friend's blogs. The prize: a beautiful photograph of the Empire State Building. I'd always imagined visiting there with my future husband. Ever since I first saw "Sleepless in Seattle" as a little girl. Recently, I'd watched "An Affair to Remember" and cried at the tragic tale. It was all so romantic.

I won the giveaway and received the beautiful print in the mail. I hung it on my wall, above my desk where I blogged and worked.

Every time I looked at it, it was like a symbol, a little sign between me and my God.

That He saw, He heard, He knew.

And He had not forgotten.

Venice, Italy

Daniel took his viola and went out on the streets of Maryland, performing wherever he could. Rain or shine. He intended to make it his career, to make money at it, however he could.

Busking on the street, humbly, he played eight to ten hours every day. He slept in his truck at a gas station, curled up in the cab in the freezing cold. He'd brush his teeth in the gas station bathroom, buy and eat a gas station croissant, and then go out and play, again.

Fearless and fighting for what he dreamed of. He would make it work. Sometimes he performed at weddings, and several opportunities arose in music.

That spring, his sister Anna came to visit and the two took a trip to New York City for a day.

Atop the Empire State Building, they stood, looking out over the city.

Daniel's mind raced as he looked over the vastness. He thought of all the millions of people out in the world, and thought: "She's out there, somewhere."

He began to pray for his future wife, as he had for years and years. All he could think of in that moment, standing up above the world looking out over New York City was his girl…where was she?

He began to pen a song:

"Sometimes I thought I found you
But God said, 'No, I've got someone better.'
So I guess I'm still waiting for that day when
I'll hold you in my arms

So baby, know you're not alone
'Cause wherever I go
You'll be right by my side
In my prayers every night
I'll be praying for you
And I'll be thinking of you and imagining who you
are
I know I'll wake up someday with you in my arms
But until that day comes you're in my heart
And I'll be praying for you

Sometimes the road was so tough
And my heart broke
I could barely go on
Sometimes I was lonely and yes I cried
Sometimes I thought I could hear you
Hear you say

Baby, know you're not alone
'Cause wherever I go
I'll be right by your side, you're in my prayers every
night
And I'll be praying for you

And when that day comes and I'm holding you
I will look into your eyes and I'll say

Baby, know you're not alone 'cause wherever I go
I'll be right by your side, you're in my prayers every
night
So I'll be praying for you and thinking of you
As I'm holding you in my arms
I know I'll wake up someday with you by my side
But until that day comes, you're in my heart
And I'm praying for you."

Little did I know, every day when I looked at my
photograph hanging on the wall, he was praying for
me… thinking of me, too. Standing on that very
Empire State Building.

Oh, little did I know.

Months later, a lanky young man sat on a bus bench.
He carefully tied his gray backpack to the silver pole
and laid down to sleep.

Daniel had recovered from his depression, thank the
Lord. He felt so good, so alive, so much *better.*

He went shooting out of his depression like a rocket into orbit, into a kind of mania.

Full of life and dreams, he raced ahead, full speed, pursuing his dream of music, head on.

It was a hot, humid August and he had to get out of Maryland, travel and see the world.

Be wild and free!

He booked a flight to Switzerland and landed in Geneva.

He spent a week in the breathtaking Alps.

Then two days in Venice, Italy. It was romantic, charming, and quaint, perfect for lovers. But, alas, he was alone.

Down the coast of Italy.

Across the Adriatic Sea to Greece.

Up to Macedonia and Serbia – thinking he was in Romania. (Accidently taking the wrong train.)

Over to Budapest, Hungary.

And into Vienna, Austria. (A cornucopia of music history.)

Sleeping in train stations. Staying in hostels. Eating croissants and Danishes. Drinking coffee and European beer.

Up to Prague. Across Germany.

And then to Amsterdam. The Netherlands. Holland.

Back down to Brussels, Belgium.

Then down to a rainy Paris. (sadly, he didn't have anyone to kiss.) He asked a local man where the sun was. He told him to follow the sun to the southern coast.

He followed it to Marseille, France.

Then scuba diving in coastal Nice. And to Cremona, where Stradivarius violins were crafted.

Back up through Italy, to Lucerne, Switzerland, and again to Geneva.

Then, home to America.

The adventure of a lifetime.

Unforgettable.

I opened my hope chest. I hadn't even looked in it for a year. I couldn't. It hurt, bad. It literally mocked me; the wooden lid perched open like a mouth, laughing at me. I swear I saw it.

Those baby clothes, all wrapped up neatly. I rolled my eyes.

The wedding scrapbook stickers. Ugh.

A pink cutting board. Gross.

The cream colored dishes. Knife to my heart.

Part of me cringed. Part of me longed. Part of me felt sick.

Half of me wanted to throw it all out my bedroom window.

While the other half wanted to take each item tenderly in my hands and smell its cedar scent (it was permeated, because, let's face it: the stuff had been in there for nearly ten years) and cry a thousand tears.

It felt like loss, oddly.

A special and very real loss; loss of something you've never had. There is no word in the English language for this kind of loss. In other languages, there are words for this kind of emptiness. I couldn't think of one, but it was just as keen and real.

The kind of "loss" that makes you feel dumb, achy, and left out.

And scared.

Instead, I decided to go all Monica from *Friends* on my Hope Chest and take out every item, dust it off, and list it in order. Might as well get it all organized, right? Know what I had?

"1. Light pink bird house.
  2. Blue baby booties.
  3. "Emma" cake stand.
  4. Pink stitched napkin"

And then, I saw it.

Oh, the dread. The horror. The literal gasp that came from my lips.

The fabric on some of my items was *disintegrating*.

Yep. Disintegrating.

And yellowing over.

Like my grandma-in-heaven's trunk of keepsakes.

That's how long I'd been waiting?

Dang. It was horrifying, to say the least.

That's how *old maid*. An old maid?!

I was a grandma. Well, a grandma who really can't ever be *called* a grandma because, ha! Well, you are just an old lady maid if you never have any kids. And my clock was ticking. Fast. This just proved i! In a real-life, real-time picture. And it sucked. Hard.

To think! I'd bought items in hopes for my future husband and family and home almost a *decade* ago. And those items had been sitting in a cedar chest, waiting right along with me, for ten long years? So long that their fabric became yellowed without any human contact or sunlight or love? And here they were, right along with their dreadfully pitiful owner, sitting in Mom and Dad's house and oh, I'm almost *thirty*? "Holy freaking crap."

I had to sit down.

It was sobering, to say the least.

My hands shaking, I let the heavy wooden lid down crash with a thud.

Suffice it to say, my hope chest stayed shut from that day on and that afternoon marks the first real moment when I was *this* close to actually throwing its contents out the window. I literally almost did it.

But, yet? Hope. I still had that hope. It was just whispering, these days.

It was still there. Though faint, whimpering, weary,

sad, and a lot discouraged. Hope.

 Little did I know, had I really gone forward and thrown it's contents out my window into the oak grove behind the house, the Lord knew that in that very spot — the spot where I had my raging meltdown over the church loss and my unrequited love seven years before-- that two years later, I would be saying "I do" to my man. He was on his way. I just didn't know it yet and very highly doubted it at the time.

Oh, the grace.

My old friend Rachel texted me that afternoon. She said,

"So, this afternoon I was vacuuming. You know. And the Lord stopped me in the middle of it. I had to step away from the vacuum and text you! He told me to tell you this. Like, I couldn't even finish my vacuuming! He *had* to have you know, Erin….

You know the old classic song 'Unforgettable' by Nat King and Natalie Cole? Well…. that is what He says to you. All those lyrics.

You are unforgettable, to Him. He has not forgotten you. You are remembered and loved.

He has *not* forgotten you, friend. You are not forgotten."

No words. Just tears.

I laid on the couch and listened to those iconic voices croon. Unforgettable? That's what I am?

How great is our God.

Part Three

COWBOY AND ME

A Love Story

Wild and Free

I am an avid journal writer. I've kept a journal of prayers and dreams, hopes and everyday happenstance nearly every day since the age of about eleven years old. And for years, I've named each journal — each season — with a fitting word or a phrase. For what I hoped it would hold. Naming what I hoped God would do in my life. A healing He would bring. A door He would open.

Autumn of 2010: "Faithful Fall."

The winter of 2012: "Fearless."

On December 19th, 2013, I started a new document "journal." It was time. My last was full to the brim — hundreds of pages and the urge for a new season welled and ached in my heart like water coming from a fire hose.

I remember sitting on my bed that night. The house was quiet, Mom and Dad long asleep. I prayed, begging for a new season. You know those times you are so weary in your season that you can't even cry about it? You can't even really be mad? You are just so tired. That was me that cold winter's night.

"Wild and Free"

The new journal's name.

I needed something new, something fresh. A breakthrough. My prayers answered. My soul felt discouraged, my heart felt disenchanted, and my mind felt very jaded and a little sarcastic even, but a thread of hope lived on, somewhere in there. And I decided this season would be wild and free. Lord willing.

I wrote the first entry:

"*December 19, 2013. 12AM. Home.*

Lord, I put my heart in Your hands and trust You with my dreams. I'm scared to. But how can I not?

You know my heart and thoughts. You know why and what I am feeling. I pray for peace. And open doors. And shut doors.

I pray something Gilmore Girl-ish exciting to happen."

"Gilmore Girlish" was my phrase over the years prior for when something crazy cool happens out of nowhere and just sweeps you off your feet. Something that only usually happens in TV land. Like when Lorelei runs into Luke at the most perfect moments. Or when Rorie just happens to meet the perfect guy her last year of school. Those two always had a lot of drama, but their lives certainly weren't boring, and they always had the most fun, exciting, interesting things happen, especially with men. Single, tired me? I just wanted that, too.

I had prayed for it one other time, right after my first breakup. After church one unusually rainy Los Angeles Sunday, I spent the afternoon in my favorite coffee shop with a couple of friends. As I stirred in a sprinkle of cinnamon on top of my chai latte I realized something: Chad Michael Murray (Tristan from *Gilmore Girls*, you know) was stirring half and half into *his* mug…. Suffice it to say, I nearly passed out. (And yes, I got a picture with him if you Gilmore fans were wondering.)

Ice Skates, Brown Boots and Matchmaking

"It can happen so fast
Or a little too late
Timing is everything.
Natalie Hemby and Troy Jones

On a wintery Sunday evening, January 29th, 2013, our lives were about to change forever.

Daniel slipped on brown boots, a black coat, and a scarf. Back home at the farm for the Christmas season, Daniel planned to go ice skating that evening with his siblings. Cindy asked the older boys in the house to line up in the new boots they'd bought while shopping that afternoon. She snapped a quick photo of them on her iPhone and posted it to her Instagram account, with this comment:

"If they come back from ice skating still single... {available: left to right Elijah, age 23. Daniel, age 26. Micah, 18.} hahahaha!!!"

Lighthearted and silly, she got a pretty enthusiastic response from many of her followers – moms matching up their daughters, interested young ladies, married friends thinking of their single ones. Some good-intentioned matchmaking commenced! Of course, I saw nothing. Because, I knew nothing of the Morris family.

But, as the Lord would have it, Cindy and I shared a

mutual friend.

When I first signed up for an Instagram account back in my early blogging days, I followed other Christian women. Amy (@amyhersheykisses) is one of the first women I connected with on the brand new app. She and I were online friends and had never met "in person" but I knew her well enough through several years of watching each other's lives through our blogs and commenting and chatting. She was a woman I trusted.

She'd noticed Cindy's photo and commented. Knowing my heart for waiting because I shared it so openly through my online ministry, she commented on Cindy's photo, saying this:

"I've been meaning to suggest to @itserinjames that @daniel_t_m is available…this seems like the perfect opportunity."

Cindy replied, "I think there could be something here!!! Haha!!!"

Daniel got back home to the farm late, logged onto Instagram, and saw the comments. He spent the rest of the evening looking through every single photo I had ever posted. He was interested, smitten.

He thought (and this is his direct quote, not mine): *"This girl is so attractive! Model status. And after looking at her posts, her heart is just as attractive. Man, this is the kind of girl I would wanna be with but there's no way. So unlikely that she would wanna be with me. I don't really think there is a chance..."*

And he reasoned, *"No.... This couldn't work out. I don't know her! I live in Maryland; she lives in California."*

Despite his family's encouragement, he felt cautious. But... he decided "to give it a try."

I, on the other hand - missed *all of it.* Randomly that evening, one of my Instagram followers "liked" *every single one* of my photos. Because news feeds only show a certain amount of comments, likes, and new follows, Amy's "tag" on Cindy's photo was so far down in my news feed, I did not ever see it. What I *did* see late that Sunday evening as I was turning on the shower with one hand and holding my phone and scrolling through Instagram with the other-- was a new follower...@daniel_t_m.

Daniel Morris.

My Instagram account was not private, being a blogger. *Most* of my new followers are strangers to me. Yet, this guy seemed so out of the blue - he wasn't a blogger and nor was he a teenage girl. Most of my new followers at the time were. In a quick check through his profile, I noticed we shared *no* mutual followers or follows.

He's handsome. I thought.

And plays violin? Whoa. Never met a young guy who does that.

And, full disclosure? As I scrolled through the snapshots of this random guy's beachy, musical and sometimes shirtless photos, my other thought was: *nice abs.*

But, I did not follow him back. He was a stranger.

I turned off my phone, hopped in the shower, and then went off to bed.

On December 30th, 2013, I woke up to sunlight streaming through my window. I pulled myself up in bed and grabbed my iPhone from my bedside table. Rubbing my eyes and yawning, my hair in a messy bun atop my head, I mindlessly tapped on Instagram. Wow, I had *a lot* of notifications! *What are all these comments?*

About ten comments popped up from a lady named Cindy on an older photo I'd posted a week ago. The photo, an encouraging print that read:

"In God's timing, He restores everything in ways so good you could not dream them up yourself."

I thought the comments were most likely from a girl asking for advice, or sharing her heart, asking about my book, or telling me how thankful she was that I wrote about waiting because her daughter was touched… the kinds of long comments I typically received on Instagram. But no… what was this? I tapped and read through her words and my heart began to pound. Dread washed over me.

No. I thought.

This person is trying to match me up with some guy?! Oh great.

Honestly, I rolled my eyes, annoyed.

Being a twenty-seven-year-old Christian woman who blogged about waiting for Mr. Right, I *very often* got "matched up." Everybody and their mom, with well-meaning and kind hearts, tried to play cupid with me and their "precious grandson," "adorable cousin," "godly son," or "cute brother."

I always appreciated their efforts, but one thing was certain in my heart of hearts: yes, I am a blogger but no, my future husband *will not be found on the Internet.* I always, quickly and graciously turned these down without blinking an eye. Plus, in my current season and state of mind at the time, I wrote most guys off – at the drop of a hat. My standards were higher than Mount Everest and my heart as guarded as Air Force One. Picky and even overly careful, I was not really open to dating anymore. My heart felt tender. And finding a man via the Internet, of all places? Not my current idea of fun.

But, as I read Cindy's words, I couldn't help myself. I smiled, spontaneously. Her words seemed humble and genuine. Warm and open. She didn't seem pushy, creepy, or weird as random strangers online could potentially be. Just pure *love* for her boy… her son, and the Lord, seeped out of her words.

She wrote:

"Hi Erin, I don't know if you noticed that amyhersheykisses tagged you in a photo I posted on IG. I like to have fun with my guys but also God does use 'means!' I've known Amy through IG for several years and love her to pieces! Anyway, you know moms, they like to go behind the scenes sometimes!! We have 13 children, 9 boys and 4 gals, two sets of twins. We live in the country in Oklahoma, and have a small farm, have homeschooled all of our children, and still homeschooling!! Ha!! Our oldest are twins. Caleb is married (1 ½ years) and has our first grandson. Daniel, the second born twin is 26, 27 in August. He's the one Amy tagged you about. One reason I am even writing you a note is, that's how Caleb, the first born and his wife met, a random her being a wedding photographer, her contacting us about taking photos of our family and sharing our journey with our 11th son, a twin at three years old who died of cancer in Jan 07. She flew out here from Maryland and we didn't know her from Eve but they fell in love and were married! This is crazy I know but… anyway, Daniel is 26, he asked Jesus in his heart at age 6. He has sought to live and "wait" and keep himself for that one, he started playing the piano at age 6 and the viola at age 16. Music is his passion and has played at many notable places, like the Italian embassy in DC. He actually lives in MD. Of all our children, he is the most compassionate about people and serving others. His gift is service. He recently traveled to Europe by himself, played his

viola on the streets and toured for a month just for fun. All of our sons have worked for my husband who has our own construction company. He is here now for a visit and has been working with Terry my husband and we have enjoyed having him here. I'm a little nervous for doing this, but like I said when Kristen, (oldest sons now wife) when she came that one time, I started texting her and of course Caleb wanted to get to know her and so that's that. My husband has taught our children well in the truth, that God is sovereign, he directs and orders our paths and that all things happen for our good and his glory. We have sought to teach them all the importance of keeping themselves for that one God has for them and so far they have honored that. I have enjoyed looking at your photos and the godly, enjoyable, encouraging life that you lead. Hope this all wasn't too out there but like I said, sometimes, a mom just has instincts. Ha!! Thanks for reading this if you do and would love to hear back from ya!!"

I sat straight up in bed. Butterflies filled my stomach, and then I rolled my eyes.

I cannot be hurt again. I whispered to myself.

"I hate being matched up." I said, inwardly.

Mom opened my door, came into my room and sat down at my desk.

"Mommmmmm…." I whined.

"Some blogger woman found my Instagram and commented that I should *marry her son.* It is *such* a nightmare. I am *not* responding."

She smiled and her eyes widened.

She asked more.

We looked at Cindy's profile. Oh my gosh.

I saw that she had posted something the night before. I was tagged in it! We tapped on the photo of Daniel, Elijah, and Micah, on their way out the door to ice skate.

Getting ready to take Mom and Dad (as planned) to Bakersfield to run errands, I noticed Cindy had posted another photo that morning. Daniel, with his little sister – and the comment: "Just a re-post, for various reasons!!!! Ha! And hey, what a fun thread last night on the three guys. I was laughing so hard!!! #mommasuptosomething."

I almost died.

Panicking, yes, panicking. I felt like I couldn't breathe.

On the drive with my parents, I chattered like a monkey, listing reasons why I should *not* respond to this woman. Mom and Dad listened patiently.

Later that morning, Amy sent me a private message on Instagram. She told me how carefully she chose to tag me and Daniel in that comment. She is not a silly, teasing or flippant lady by any means. I knew if she thought of this young man as a potential "match" for me it would be unwise, unkind, and just plain stupid of me *not* to at least be open to the *possibility.*

As my parents shopped, I found a Starbucks and sat at a small wooden table, alone. I ordered a Grande Caramel Macchiato. I turned country music on my headphones and looked through every single one of Cindy and Daniel's photos. And then, I opened my laptop and found her blog.

I read and looked at pictures. They drew me in, I couldn't deny it.

The big Walton-like family of thirteen.

And they lived on a farm? I loved farms.

I read about Daniel. There was something about a depression. I wondered. I understood.

I wanted to know more.

I read about their family's desire to honor and follow the Lord. Tears fell down my face as I read the story of sweet *Joel*.

Coffee grinders grinding and people chatting.... and I sat there, engrossed. And I knew: *these people are the real deal.*

From the photos I scrolled through on her blog, I gathered bits and pieces of him. His story. His heart. He seemed to have land he saved for and a house he designed? I saw a photo of him pouring cement. Daniel wrote: "Daniel + Wife" encircled with a heart in the wet cement. Oh, how sweet.

I "stalked" him on Google, finding his music YouTube channel. That coffee shop. That moment when I first pressed *play* on his video and heard his music. Someday, when I am old and sitting in a rocking chair, reminiscing and musing on the best days of my life, I *will* remember that moment.

I clicked on his videos, one after another: beautiful viola and piano. I sat with my earbuds in and the volume turned up. I listened. I played it again.

And my heart? Entirely overwhelmed.

I had to turn it off. I pressed pause.

I sat and tried to breathe. His skill level: like a virtuoso.

And his heart? Oh, I could feel it.

Later that night, I wrote in my journal:

"There is something about the way he plays. With so much expression and passion. I cried. I said aloud: 'This is too much to handle.' I watched him play, with so much feeling... more

than anyone I had ever seen. The song went on and on, passion pouring from his fingertips onto the keys."

That night, I watched more videos on my laptop.

I wept.

It was healing, somehow.

In my faithful journal, I wrote:

"... and there is something about his eyes. They are beautiful and sad and wild and alive. Like they hold the whole history of the world in them. I have never in my life seen someone with such beautiful, deep, expressive, pure blue eyes. Ever. I could drown in his eyes. I am NOT KIDDING."

I replied to Cindy's comments. I couldn't help myself.

"Awww you and @amyhersheykisses are the sweetest ever! What an amazing family, & your son sounds like a great guy. I am always up for meeting people who have similar hearts! Thanks for saying hi!"

New Year's Eve, 2013, came.

A response from Cindy: "Oh my gosh oh my gosh!!!! Thanks for getting back to me!!! Hahaha!! I was like a little excited to hear back! How fun. Anyways, I will enjoy being your new IG fan!!!!"

And no word from him.

Hmmmm. I thought. *I guess nothing will come of it, after all.*

Never a pursuer of guys, I knew that if we were to start talking, he would need to be the initiator.

That Daniel Morris. On my mind.

But, that was that.

I let it go.

And then, he initiated. On New Year's Eve.

Commenting on Instagram.

And I died.

He was calm, cool, friendly, not creepy, sincere, and obviously maybe-kind of interested. A pretty perfect combination. He commented on an older, black and white picture of me, playing the piano.

Comment one: "Would love to hear some music"

And comment two: "I'm assuming you might know who I am haha, considering that some people have been doing some things behind the scenes. Lol. Just wanted to say hi and keep up all the encouraging stuff you're posting on here."

I called Mom and Dad into my room.

Immediately, I called Mandy. She was shopping at the grocery store with Dot.

I told her everything. I sent her pictures of him I found on Facebook. I sent her a screen shot of his comments.

She hesitated for 3 seconds and then she very purposefully said:

"Sis."

"He is a *ten*. He looks exactly like Robert Redford *and* he is a cowboy!"

And then, loud and clear through the phone, I heard her speak (in her most serious, bossy voice I know she only uses when she means business and you better listen up)

"Sis.... *Do not screw this up.*"

So.... I replied.

Openly. Kind. Friendly.

And he replied.

Butterflies.

For the first time in a long time.

Over New Year's Eve night and New Year's Day, 2014, we commented back and forth on my picture. We talked of music. And life. My book. His viola. His album.

Every time a comment of his popped up on my notifications, my heart leapt and my face flushed.

Daniel spent New Year's Eve spontaneously driving from Maryland to New York City, he and Elijah, Anna and a friend.

I spent New Year's Eve at home with Mom, Dad, Mandy, and Rachel. We watched the ball drop on TV. When I saw Daniel's photo on Instagram in Times Square, I realized we were watching where he was.

It was a sweet night. We worshipped on guitar and piano and at midnight, we popped some bubbly and toasted to a new year. I told 2013 and all its sorrows to let itself out the back door. It felt like a new season; good and somehow *really fresh*. Rachel and Dad kept teasing me about "Mr. Viola." I said, "Noooo, he's not my guy!" They laughed and teased all the more.

On New Year's Day mom made fried chicken. We went to Malibu Beach. Something in my heart began to flutter. Daniel commented again. And I felt alive, somehow.

"**@itserinjames:** yeah, I do know who you are haha! Thanks, I'm getting ready to put some music up soon, my sis & I sing together. I'd love to hear your music!"

Although, let's face it, I already had.

"**@daniel_t_m:** haha yeah well funny how things happen sometimes, I guess. That's so cool. Are you putting out an album?"

"**@daniel_t_m:** I am working on releasing one soon. It's all recorded. Just working on the production part of it."

"**@itserinjames**: yeah :) recording is our goal for 2014! We did a lot as kids & are getting back into it. Wow that's exciting! Where can I hear a recording of your music?"

"**@daniel_t_m:** that's great! Are you going to a studio? Or doing it yourself? Yeah pretty happy to have the tracks laid down. Now if we can just get it wrapped up. And we haven't released it yet so it's not up anywhere. But here's little sneak peek just for you." *(And he added a link.)*

"**@itserinjames:** thanks! We are planning to do it in a studio but it's all kind of a dream right now! I'm actually self-publishing a book for my blog readers currently, so I'm trying to finish up & then work on the record this year. Aw thanks for sharing it with me! Oh my word, your music is absolutely beautiful, just lovely!!! Your album's going to be amazing. Happy

New Year's Eve :)"

"**@daniel_t_m:** Aw thanks so much! Glad you like it and the link actually worked. Wow that's so amazing that you wrote a book. Probably so much work in doing it yourself. And well if when you get ready I have a hook up to a studio. If you want to come to D.C. :) I think you could get it done for free!! And make that dream become a reality. Happy New Years. It's going to be an awesome year."

"**@itserinjames:** oh yes the link worked & it was so beautiful, loved it. Thank you, yeah it's a crazy journey of writing. Awww, that's amazing, really? I've always wanted to visit D.C. – only been to the East Coast on layovers :) Happy New Year! I saw your pic in Times Square, how awesome was it to celebrate there?!"

@daniel_t_m: Awesome glad you liked it :) What is your book written about? And yeah, I'm serious about the studio out here. You should come out for real! I'll show you around and we'll get your album recorded :) Times Square was incredible. We got a super spot. Not without some adventure getting there lol. But we did it. Hey do you have an email or some way we could communicate? Haha. Or we could just keep this thread going forever."

Oh, my heart. Forever?

"**@itserinjames:** That would be so fun :) thanks for

asking about the book – I have a blog for young gals & so the book is like the blog, just my heart & story, sharing encouragement in an honest, coffee date kinda style about how to live life as a Christian woman in this crazy world. Ah that must have been so awesome to be in Times Square, how great you got a super spot!! An adventure I'm sure. Haha. Yes this could become the longest thread ever :) it's – erinjames@hotmail.com."

I spent New Year's Day on a very summery, warm Malibu beach, with a latte in one hand, a journal in the other, and my family by my side. We were on opposite ends of the country.

I thought and prayed, all day, as I sat on the beach. My phone died so I couldn't reply to him. I walked along the sand… the waves coming up every minute, licking my feet. The water was freezing. I prayed. I gave it to the Lord even though I was too scared to say it, to acknowledge it.

I was dying over this guy. I later wrote in my journal:

"He seems so cute and sweet. And, like a MAN. Which, I have never encountered. Ever. I have also picked apart every single thing he wrote to find something wrong. Something offensive or not strong enough or man enough. He's perfect.

We took our conversation to email.

It was all very "You've Got Mail" of us.

He asked for my email on January 1, 2014. He emailed me for the first time on January 2.

Talk about a New Year! It really felt like it.

"Hey Erin! It's Daniel. Well I guess we can email now haha. That's so exciting about your book. I have seen a little of your blog. It seems like you really have a great ministry to girls with that. I can only imagine where the book will take it. This world is so crazy these days. So many pressures that the world puts on girls. I think what you are doing is awesome. Godly Christian women are hard to find. The coffee date real type of setting, just sharing your heart, is really cool. Love it.

Yeah the energy and excitement there in New York was crazy. So much fun…."

He told me all about Times Square and the adventure that night led him on.

He signed off,

"Daniel"

Sent from my iPhone.

My heart felt warm. I was honestly impressed. He was intentional, sweet, kind, thoughtful, and not creepy.

Win. Somehow, he was all those things in one. I was surprised. He was detailed and told me things. And something that *really* struck me, even from a few comments and *one* email? He talked less about himself and more about me.

The guys I had known and dated were all about *them*. They never asked about me.

They didn't care about my music, passion, dreams, writing or my heart. They just cared that I was pretty.

But he? He was different.

I liked him. Even as just a friend, I told Mom. She *lit up* when I showed her. Mandy was floored. She said she could not believe there was a sweet guy who was real and actually talked to a girl, and was respectful.

I painstakingly figured out what to reply. And I said this:

On January 2, 2014, at 9:33 PM.

"Hey Daniel!

Aw, thank you, what you said about the blog and book – your encouragement meant a lot. As an artist, I'm sure you know what it's like to put your heart and yourself out there and it can be hard at times, so thank you.

Haha oh wow! That sounds like such an adventure! So awesome that you got to be right down by the concert stage where you could see the ball. What a fun experience! :) How fun that you got in!"

I told him that I looked up his music on YouTube, and that it was just so beautiful, it made me cry. I asked all about it. I told him that I'd been in a hard season, lately, and that music hadn't been a part of my life for years, but that I thought the Lord was bringing it back… because, He redeems things.

And so it went.

Emails back and forth. He spent the first days of 2014 in snowy New York City, exploring and spending time with his whole family. They now tell me that every night, after everyone went to bed, Daniel sat crouched in the corner over his iPhone for hours, painstakingly and carefully writing out these emails to me. He refreshed his Gmail app on coffee breaks that week, waiting for a reply from that girl out in California. 2,780 miles away.

One evening as they explored NYC , the Morris family piled out of the freezing cold streets and into John's on Bleeker Street, a pizzeria. The room was full of wooden walls covered in happily carved "graffiti" – lover's names – "I was here!" – remembrances, all etched with forks and knives, and haphazardly scribbled all over benches and tables.

The Morris family settled into tables and booths and Daniel had an idea.

He picked up a silver butter knife and found an open space on the side of his bench.

"What can it hurt?" He thought.

"It may work out…maybe not. But it just feels – right."

And so, he carved. Amid all the other scribbles and lover's names:

"D A N" and "E R I N" in the dark wood.

And then…. half a heart – a question mark.

If he ever met this girl across the country. This California girl. If it worked out. If we might-possibly, maybe fall in love…. Someday. He would take her there.

And carve the question mark half-heart into a full heart.

Maybe someday.

Daily, we exchanged emails. My heart leapt into my throat every time I heard the *ding!* and saw his name in my inbox. His emails were long and wordy, warm and open… and then, a little flirty.

Guys used to ask me, often – "Sooo, you blog? And you're a freelance writer? What is your *real job?*"

It always felt like slap in the face to me because…um, that was my real job, my dream. I had sacrificed for it, was not making loads of cash, but working my tail off for it. But Daniel?

In one of his long, sweet emails, he asked – gingerly and sensitively: "How amazing that you have a blog! Are you able to blog and share and write books full-time?"

His carefulness and respect for my dream chasing? It meant a lot to me and spoke volumes about his values, his heart and his sensitivity. His kindred wild and free spirit.

We talked of music, and his time at YWAM. The Ranch. Of our families and best friend siblings. We talked about big dream chasing. Our relationships with Jesus.

In one email he said, "Well I am so excited to meet someone with the same heart for dreaming and going after it for the Lord too. Never give up because it's so worth it. Even though there are those times, like you said, that you're thinking, 'What the heck am I doing?' We will get somewhere – if God is for us who can be against us!

We need to work out meeting sometime. Haha.

Although we are on opposite sides of the US. That's no biggy."

And he signed off with: "Have a great Sunday!

Love hearing from you.

Daniel"

In my journal, I copied and pasted our emails. And I wrote: "But seriously… is he not the MOST precious? Sweetest? KINDRED SPIRIT? DREAMER? LIKE WOAH.

Truly, everything he writes and everything I've found out about him through his mom's blog, his Facebook, and YouTube….makes me swoon.

And Mandy's right. He does look like ROBERT freaking REDFORD."

I read the family blog about how he worked hard for their construction company, saving money for the land and dreaming of buying it for his future home and family and wife. How he bought it. How he drew up a dream house, in faith, for his future wife. And in my journal I wrote, "GASP. TEARS. SHOCK. HYPERVENTILATE! I MUST BE DREAMING! I died when I saw the photos and read it all. Swooned. It was too much. It IS too much. It's only been a week and a day and I am falling. And I don't want to. And tonight, I sit alone in my bed with my cat. Shorts on and a big t-shirt, and a pounding heart.

And I care.

And, I didn't want to!

Ugh, I hate this. I have a crush on him now! And I don't care about anyone else I have ever liked or admired or seen. I am beginning to fall for this beautiful man, not even because of how he looks or how he plays music, but for his heart on paper. I have seen enough to know how precious he is. How rare.

And it scares the crap outta me. What if! What IF!!!!!!!!!!!!!

I am not just a passionate lover of anyone I fall for. But I see myself falling for him. And you know what? This is JUST the beginning. I can see it.

He is precious. And someone I feel I could maybe give my heart to and place my life in his hands."

The hope of it all was very sweet, very sweet.

And to my journal and the Lord, I wrote:

"But Lord… what is your plan? Who *is* this beautiful man you brought to my path on literally like January 1? It's too much. It's also really sweet. And sooooo exciting. But I am scared. More scared than I've ever been. To lose him. I cannot lose more. I have not yet gotten over the loss of the last year alone. And I cannot do more yet. Lord, come. Direct my heart. Guard it, for now.

Keep me strong and confident and wise.

And for Daniel, I pray for wisdom too. For direction.

'In the Lord's hand the King's heart is a stream of water directed by the Lord; He directs it wherever He pleases.' – *Proverbs 21:1.*

Direct his heart and give him wisdom. Show him how to pursue me. And if to. Open my heart to him and whatever You might be doing. Guard it from what you may not be. If this is a no, please be gentle with me. I cannot handle much. You know that.

Are we to meet? Open the door. Are we to date? Open the door. May it be effortlessly easy if it is meant to be. I pray for happy things, laughter, dates, kisses, and good things. If it is meant to be. And for extra measures of grace, if it is not.

Open doors and remember all my old prayers."

All I Know Is We Said Hello

"What if I fall?"
"Oh, my darling,
*   what if you fly?"*

On January 11th, 2014, Daniel emailed me back. And in the long, wordy, thoughtful flirty email he said, "Would you be down to talk on the phone? Might be a little easier to get to know each other. I much prefer in person and I'm not a big on the phone person. But just emailing is getting old fast haha…. So maybe, if you're down, I can get your number :)"

He asked to talk on the phone. Gasp!

On the evening of the 12th, we talked on the phone for the very first time. Before he called, I was in a frenzy, my heart pounding and mind racing.

I lit a candle and sat down at my pink desk.

I took my Bible from my bedside table, opened it up, and it fell open to the book of Daniel! It was marked by a little blue sticky note I wrote back in college, in 2010.

Under the book of the Bible "Daniel," the blue sticky note with red handwriting read,

"Do not fear. Only believe." Mark 5:16.

Peace.

The phone rang.

Mandy texted me about twenty-five pink heart emojis and eight kissy lips. She wrote, "I'm shaking omg. I'm praying Boo. You'll be great this is funnnnn!"

I quickly typed back, "He's so sweet & nervous lol."

She responded: "Yeyyyyyyyyyyyyy"

Our conversation lasted three hours.

We talked about life. Our stories. His depression. The Ranch. The Farm. Being homeschooled. Jesus. Travel. Adventures. Music. Writing. Dreaming big. Being wild and free.

And it was *all over* when I heard his warm, shaky, excited, "Heyyyy..." colored with a southern accent. It was like I'd known him all my life.

He texted me right after we got off the phone.

I'd put his name in my cell phone as "Daniel Cowboy" – because of his accent. He grew up on an Oklahoma farm. That's what Mandy and I called him – because he reminded her so much of Clint Eastwood in an old cowboy movie.

If I was honest with myself in those beginning days, I

was very, very scared.

When you start to fall – you know, and it is thrilling but scary.

One night during our second week of talking, he didn't text all day long.

And I started to freak out.

A thousand what- ifs raced through my head. The sun went down. Still no word. Should I text first? Should I wait? (Oh, girls, I understand the texting limbo at the beginning of a new relationship. The struggle is real.)

Living on a mountaintop, iMessage was my mode of texting. Regular "texts" did not come through, because I only had Internet – no cell service or data.

I decided he must have sent me a message via "text." That means I wouldn't get it, not until I drove down the mountain where my cell had service.

Rain fell lightly and the air was cool and damp that night. I jumped in the car and tore down the wet mountain road. Screeching down the hairpin turns, flying around the curves as the black asphalt shined in the headlights.

I was desperately afraid of being hurt.

And by someone so exquisite.

I've never met him. I would whisper to Mom.

Is this crazy?! We have never met in person! What if he never wants to? And just keeps texting me for who-knows-how-long? What if he just seems normal but in person he is insane? What if he never writes back? And I'm left hanging and humiliated? What if he never wants to call me or meet me?

Oh, but what if it does?

My cell phone always got service again at the Ranch, just three miles up the mountain road from our home. I pulled into the east entrance gate, beside the white fence by my beloved, big white barn. It looked so shabby compared to how it stood years ago in shining glory in its heyday, when I lived there. Its paint was now chipping off, brown wood showing through. Shaking and worried, I tapped my phone screen. Five full bars of service and 3G data. But, no messages from Daniel Cowboy. I sat there for a good fifteen minutes on the Ranch. Rain pattering down on my windshield, thick darkness all around. Tears streaming down my cheeks.

I gave him to the Lord, again. In the place where I gave Him my future husband at the beginning. Fourteen long years ago.

I drove home, slowly and sad. Yes, overdramatic and overacting (and I've never done *that* before). But, oh – my heart. On the line. And putting your heart on the line and starting to fall? It's scary.

He got in touch, later that evening. The poor man hurt himself on the construction job that day. A gash to his head. And here I was, thinking we were over.

For the rest of the month of January, we texted all day, every day and talked about once or twice a week.

On January 19th in the late evening, he texted me:

"Erin, we have to meet. I'm coming to California."

The room began to spin. I had to sit down.

I told Mom. She said, "Oh my goodness… my mind is racing."

He made plans. He booked a flight. Oklahoma to California. He asked for my dad's phone number.

He called and left him a message. Dad missed it. He let me hear it on his phone. I played it over and over, and called Mandy and played it for her over the phone. My heart skipped a beat every time I heard his voice.

The next day, he introduced himself to Dad on the phone. They chatted, and got along great. He asked Dad if it was alright if he came to visit me. If it was okay for him to stay in our home for a week.

Dad said, "Happily."

On February 4, I woke up at 7:31 AM to a text from "him."

"Word this morning!

Do not be anxious about anything, but in every situation, by prayer and petition, with thanksgiving, present your requests to God. And the peace of God, which transcends all understanding, will guard your hearts and your minds in Christ Jesus. (Philippians 4:6, 7)"

Our conversations were full of encouragement. What a good, godly man. Impressing me and inspiring me at every turn. He called me "Sweet Thing."

I blushed.

Valentine's Day was a little awkward. We'd been talking on the phone for a few weeks. We would be meeting "in person" in a few days. What to do? We didn't acknowledge the holiday. Looking back, it's hilarious. He and I texted all day, but we never said a word. Was it too soon? Would that be too much? It was going slow…but really fast, all at the same time.

The day before he arrived in California, Mom and I talked over what he would be like and how this whole week would be – and I told her, "Today feels like Christmas Eve! It really does."

As I cleaned the bathroom, spotless, that afternoon, I prayed. A strange request, but I needed a sign. I asked: "Lord, if he is 'the one' – my future husband – cause him to text me today sometime and say, 'It feels like Christmas Eve!' Then I will know. It will be our secret sign, Yours and mine."

That afternoon, Mom and I ran errands to prepare for him coming. As we headed up the road to the house, ding! A text came from Daniel Cowboy.

"It feels like Christmas Eve. When I was young. Just need to go to sleep so it gets here soon! Lol."

Tears streamed down my cheeks.

He said it.

He said it, Lord.

I told Mom. Her eyes filled with tears, too.

The End of the Waiting

"I wanted it to be you. I wanted it to be you so badly."
Kathleen Kelly, "You've Got Mail"

On February 18th, 2014, Daniel flew half-way across the United States and landed at LAX.

Mandy texted me. "Sis I can't believe you have a hot cowboy flying out from the other side of the country to see u. Wow."

I replied: "Ohmygosh. It's like my dream come true sis for the first time in my life. He's even southern which is what I've always loved."

I was entirely and completely nervous.

He arrived in Los Angeles one cool and oddly damp Tuesday night in February.

Truly, I had never felt more jittery about anything in my entire life.

Mandy texted me before she and I met to drive down. "I CANT BREATHE IM SO NERVOUS ARE U DRIVING OR AM I"

She drove.

I couldn't breathe, either.

Thank the Lord for best friend sisters who take on your sorrows and joys, and hold you up and stand by your side in the biggest moments of your life.

LAX. One of the busiest airports in the world. We didn't know, but this was our destination. Who knew. Los Angeles International Airport. A place of coming and going. Beginning and ending. Goodbyes and Hellos.

The end of the journey of our waiting.

The reward for the tears. The answer to our prayers.

The cozy log cabin with warm, welcoming firelight shining through it's small-paned windows at the end of a very long, dusty road; the place where your tired feet and aching muscles, weary soul and dirty feet can come and rest.

It was the sweetest, yet strangest thing.

But we didn't know it. Yeah, we felt it…it tasted different. I knew he was special. Something about it — I knew in my heart: this is different, Erin. This could be *it*. This is probably it.

THIS IS IT.

I'd been to LAX many times in life, leaving for adventures and trips then coming back home with memories and luggage.

But never in a million and a half years would I ever have imagined meeting my future husband — *him*, the guy, the one, my man — at Los Angeles International Airport.

Mandy and I sat at the baggage claim by the window. Shaking.

We watched the clock.

He landed.

He texted. "I landed!"

Is that him? Or is that him?

People began filing into the baggage claim.

I was losing my mind.

My heart was pounding out of my chest.

"Sis, oh my gosh. I am freaking out. I can't watch. You look for him, okay? I'm just gonna hold your hand and look down, and you just watch."

"Tell me when you see him."

She nodded. She whispered:

"Okay. Wait. Is that him? No… that guy's too short."

"Hmmmm. Well, that's not him."

"And ummm, no that's not him."

"SIS. That's him. THAT'S HIM… Sis, he's here. That's him!"

I looked up. Never again would my life ever be the same.

Erin, meet your future husband. This is it. The wait is over. You can exhale.

More than a million very lively butterflies flew around my stomach and I could hardly stand up. I had decided to wear a little striped skirt, a loose white V-neck t-shirt, and brown boots. Cute, yet breezy.

And yes, there he was.

He walked up, carrying his black viola case in one hand and his suitcase in the other. I could barely take it in.

And me oh my, he was tall!

The first thing I noticed about Daniel when we met, were his eyes. Just as had I noticed in pictures and videos online.

They were deep as the ocean, blue as the sky. My heart melted away forever.

All I know is we said, "Hello." And his eyes looked like coming home….

We side-hugged.

He smelled so good.

My insides, like mush.

I introduced him to Mandy. Goodness, I had no idea he was so tall! And handsome! And rugged. He wore these brown boots, brown pants, and a brown sweater. Not very LA. More Oklahoma. I loved that.

Oh, his chiseled face, five o'clock shadow, and sandy strawberry blonde hair that almost identically matched the shade of mine.

We found his bag and led him to the car. I drove. (Although, we all wished I hadn't. So jittery, I barely got us outta there!)

And like any red-blooded California welcoming a southerner, Mandy and I took him straight to In-N-Out.

We sat, side by side, in the plastic white booth, chatting and eating fries.

The whole night felt like a dream.

He was quiet and mysterious. And I liked him. Already.

Mom and Dad waited at home. We dropped Mandy at her house and drove an hour alone, up to our mountain.

The two of us. Me and the guy from Instagram.

Who knew?

Our California Week

There is nothing quite like meeting the love of your life for the very first time. It happens very softly, really. You don't know you're meeting him until the story unfolds. When he shows up on your doorstep, you know something is different. He's an angel. He's unlike anyone you have ever seen. But, oh how you don't know. Yet, you do.

I brought him into our house. It was dark and late. Mom had a cheery fire and candle burning. Dad spent the week before Daniel came laying honey colored wood in our guest room, making it extra special and perfect for him.

Mom and Dad hugged Daniel. They were thrilled. We sat on the couches in the big living room. I made tea with honey.

That week. It could have been a full-on disaster. He flew across the country to meet a stranger and stay at my family's house! But, it turned out to be the most perfect seven days two strangers have ever spent together.

The next morning, bright and early, we dressed for the beach and as we got ready to leave, Mom smiled and snapped a photo of us. Under his arm, I smiled. Our first picture together, ever.

We drove to Malibu. Just the two of us.

The air was warm for February.

It could have been a disaster.

It wasn't awkward, but as just-met strangers, it was new. I was so excitedly nervous, I forgot to pack a beach blanket. So we stopped at Wal-Mart on the way, and all we could find? A Duck Dynasty beach towel.

We sat on the golden sand and let the sea air blow our hair as we talked.

I told him things I didn't normally tell people. He nodded, responding quietly. Not really with words.

In the back of my mind, I kept telling myself —
"Erin, stop! You're (as usual) talking too much! You're gonna scare him off." But apparently, I just didn't listen to myself.

We sat on Uncle Si and I kept on talking about everything.

Life and loss – the hardest thing I'd ever been through – the memory that haunts me. That heartache my family went through, just last year, and the even worse one we went through, the year before. I told him things I hadn't told anyone *ever*.

It all just came bubbling up and spilling out, like water from a fountain. I couldn't control it.

He sat. Nodding and listening, intently, not saying much at all. But, I could tell – instinctively – he was listening. Maybe he didn't even fully understand all my gab and chatter, but he liked it, accepted it, and respected it. And he smiled.

The perfect balmy day. We found a quiet cove. Our two sets of footprints on the sand.

I took him up to the cliffs above the crashing waves, to see the gorgeous view. The place where Mom and Dad had hiked back in their dating, sailing days.

He held onto my hand to help me up the steep, sandy parts.

Butterflies.

We got to the top and looked over the vast Pacific Ocean: so blue, so big, so dreamy. He picked a yellow flower and put it in my hair. I literally swooned and nearly fell over.

I'll never forget how a Nike-wearing young woman hiker stopped us right at the edge of the cliff and said, "Hey, do you want me to take your picture?"

"I *know* how important these moments are."

She snapped one. I thought, "You have no idea."

We ate dinner in Paradise Cove. I asked him who he'd

dated, and he asked me. We talked about nothing at all and everything at once. We laughed and smiled, sat quietly, and watched the sun set.

A pretty perfect first day.

I was sick as a dog that week, sicker than I had been in years and years. A few all-nighters pulled to complete my recently self-published e-book, "P.S. He Loves You" combined with the sheer emotional anticipation of knowing this man from the Internet was crossing the country to come stay at my *house* took their toll on my sensitive heart and body.

But I powered through. I barely had a voice and a fever raged in my body, but I just remember feeling so alive.

On Thursday, we rode bikes all afternoon in pristine Santa Barbara – past exquisite white buildings and sailboats in the sunny harbor, and State Street, draped in those big Italian stringed lights, twinkling like fairies flying around above the streets. Life felt really, really perfect.

Daniel would spend April here. Caleb and his wife and little one had planned a month-long getaway. We biked past the house where they planned to stay. We stopped at a quaint, narrow, wooden-floored flower shop that smelled just like heaven, leaving our two bikes with baskets outside. It looked like something out of a Hallmark movie.

He bought me a heart-shaped box of sea salt caramel chocolates and we took them outside, leaning on our bikes, laughing, flirting, and popping them all in our mouths.

Oh, how I liked him.

I loved the way his eyes danced and nose wrinkled when he really, really smiled.

We spent Friday at one of my favorite coffee shops and then driving down Highway 126, stopping at fruit stands beside the road, nestled in orange groves. We tasted big fresh strawberries and pieces of mango. And we talked and talked and talked.

Later that day, we sat side by side on Mom's piano bench at the house. He played around on the keys. He looked at me, slowly, his eyes lit up, and he said, "You know, someday, maybe… I have a special song to play for you. And someday… maybe, I have something to show you in New York City."

The Catalina Express

> *"People fall in love in mysterious ways,*
> *maybe just the touch of a hand."*
> Ed Sheeran

We woke before dawn on Saturday, packed up the car and drove to Long Beach. We felt comfortable in one another's presence, now. It had just been a mere few days. A few hours, really!

But somehow, I felt I had known him a lifetime.

Being together. It just felt right.

I'd told him about Catalina Island, one of California's treasures.

Before the sun rose, we were boarding The Catalina Express ferry. We rode one hour to the island. I laid my head on his shoulder, so sick with the cold I could hardly breathe. But I wouldn't let us stay home. We had to have our adventures. We'd waited too long.

Catalina was sparkling and cool that morning. We spent the day walking around, finding beach loungers and sharing a Pina Colada. He took me to a little Greek café with an ocean view. I ordered tea and a cheese plate. We talked more. About deeper things. Our families. Struggles. Stories. His depression. Our past. Our personalities.

That evening, as the sun began to sink behind the desert hills on the island, we walked along the small streets lined with bright houses of every color, plants hanging all over them. Then, up a slope and past a baseball field. Daniel saw a garden on the map, and he wanted to take me there.

We walked until we reached a big iron gate. It was

locked.

Oh, no! We missed it! It's closed.

The garden was pretty, with desert cacti and lush, green trees.

Daniel's eyes sparkled and darted back and forth. There was no one around. He had an idea.

"Wanna break in? Would you do that with me?"

He winked.

For one second, I thought about it. And then, without hesitation, I exclaimed: "Heck yeah!"

The biggest smiled I'd ever seen spread across his beautiful face.

We looked left and right. No one around. Then, he took me by the hand and helped me climb up the spindly iron gate. I jumped over and let out a little scream, covering my mouth with my hand. Then, he hoisted himself up. We were in!

Breathless, we raced into the garden. The sun set softly over the hills, a golden light falling all around us.

We ducked beneath big trees, giggling furiously and covering our mouths. We darted between a prickly cactus and a pine tree, stopping when we thought we heard someone. Okay. All clear.

We ran, faster. And then, he took my hand….

All the blood rushed to my head. And our giggling now turned to laughing. Not just sneaky-laughing, but happy laughing – very, very, happy laughing.

It started as a platonic-type hand hold. And then? I moved my fingers to intertwine with his, *really* holding hands.

Adrenaline raced through me. Because, we just broke into a locked, closed public garden! And, because I was holding hands with the man who would become the love of my life.

Finally.

Could this moment be real? It was all too wonderful.

At the top of the garden, a stone fortress was perched – high above, overlooking the island out to the sea. We wanted in, but it looked from afar as though the doors were locked.

As we moved closer, hiding in shadows as we went, I saw that the left side metal door hung open. It was bolted open, in fact. And all I could think of was: "He opens doors no one can shut, and He shuts doors no one can open." A picture, right here. That word from years ago.

His promises were coming true.

We raced up the gray stone steps, connected by our hands.

When we made it to the top, we caught the sunset. Again.

All purple and yellow and pink, and the blue ocean in the distance. Somehow, it felt like we were in a big stone castle on this island, in our very own secret garden. No one knew where we were. It was all so romantic and dreamy.

Daniel turned toward me, still holding my small hand in his big, strong one. He said, "Do you want to dance?"

We danced. Like Mr. Darcy and Elizabeth Bennett, his arm around me, twirling me around, dipping me down. We laughed and smiled, the world at our feet in that moment.

In our castle tower in our secret garden, fit for a prince and princess.

As we raced out of the now-dark garden, climbed over the big iron gates, and made it back out onto the road, we couldn't stop laughing. Or holding hands. We stopped on the way back to the ferry and ate authentic dollar tacos on the side of the road, twinkle lights sparkling above us.

It hit me. I was living my very own fairytale.

On our ride home on the Catalina Express, Daniel laid his head on my shoulder and fell asleep. My heart beat a little faster. Holding his hand, I felt electricity. It was Unlike anything I'd ever felt before in my life.

The next morning, we woke up all swoony and happy. It was Sunday and I brought him to church and then to lunch to meet Dot and my aunt Vicci. My family was wide eyed, yet smiling and surprised, when Daniel and I walked into church – hand in hand.

That night at my family's home, we went out when the sky turned velvety black.

Normally, I was scared to venture into the blackness for fear of coyotes prowling around, but he took me by the hand and we snuck out to adventure.

We ran out into the darkness, under the leafy oak trees. That week in February was unseasonably cold at my house. Windy and chilly, the thin mountain air stung my face as we walked down the gravel driveway. We found a spot under some pine trees and laid, side by side, in the dry leaves. No clouds in the sky that night, and not a street lamp in sight.

The stars shone, brightly. Twinkling.

I saw a shooting star. And then another.

"Make a wish." He whispered.

I squeezed his hand. And in my mind, I wished….

I wished that I could marry him.

Please, Lord?

It was really more of a prayer than a wish.

A Promise

Monday. Our very last day.

We didn't plan the week much. We just went and did, explored and saw, making decisions on the spur of the moment. I wanted to show him everything.

But somehow, we caught every single beach sunset. No matter what, that week.

It was magic.

We drove down to Santa Monica and I took Daniel to Huckleberry, my favorite café. It was already late afternoon, but that week we had no sense of time. We just hopped in the car and went, lost in each other's eyes.

Laguna Beach was on our itinerary of ideas. "Do you just wanna go?" I asked. We drove through rush hour traffic in the evening all the way to Laguna, chatting along the way.

It just felt so right with him by my side. And almost one week in, I knew there was something about this Oklahoma cowboy that I would never, ever get over.

Sunset. We made it to Laguna, somehow, on time to watch it. We parked and he pulled his viola out of the back of the car. He took me by the hand and we raced over the sand out to the clear blue waves, the sun setting all pink and yellow behind us, his eyes sparkling. We slipped off our shoes and he nodded, "Come on…"

Stepping on dark jutting rocks, he led me – holding tightly to my hand – further, further, further out. The tide was coming in, the waves crashing all around and still we went. My heart skipped a beat. What was he planning?

He whisked me out to a jagged rock, far past the shoreline. We stood, barefoot and shaky, with this all-consuming, head to toe "spark" and romance whirling all around us, on that rock. It felt like we were out *in the middle of the ocean,* just the two of us. Waves crashed wildly, and a hot pink round sun and pale yellow and baby blue sky surrounded us, painted by God's very own hand.

He whipped out his alluring viola and played love songs for me… while the waves crashed, and the sun sank – the sky painted brilliantly around and above us. The earth stopped spinning and it was just us.

So this is what it feels like to literally fall head first, fearless, in love.

He played a soft, sweet rendition of "Somewhere Over the Rainbow."

I couldn't breathe.

"This song is called 'The Rose' and I want to treat you like a rose, because you are special."

He then began to play the most beautiful sound I'd ever heard.

Tears.

I literally swooned. My legs became like jelly! He held me up.

I truly and literally went "weak at the knees."

Standing together on that rock, holding each other, for a long time, we didn't kiss. Although, I thought we might. But no. We didn't speak a word. We barely breathed.

With his arms around me, holding me close, we watched the sun dip beneath the blue crystal all around us.

In the darkness, he led me back to the car. Taking his phone, he said, softly, "I want to read you the lyrics to 'The Rose.'"

He read them and my heart flipped in my chest, as we stood underneath the palm trees by the sea.

When he read the last few verses, tears filled my eyes.

"When the night has been too lonely
And the road has been too long
That you think that love is only
For the lucky and the strong

Just remember in the winter
Far beneath the bitter snows
Lies the seed that with the sun's love
In the spring becomes the rose."

Six days, that's all it took. To begin to fall in love with Daniel Morris.

The waiting was so long and the lives led apart were so separate, that when the Lord finally brought us together, it just clicked. It was "it."

That evening, we found Peppertree Lane, one of the sweetest little spots in Laguna. A cozy, brick-lined walkway with arched doorways throughout, covered in tiny twinkle lights, vines and greenery, and complete with a whimsical peppertree growing up out and up in the middle. A spindly staircase leading up on one side to a grand apartment above with white shutters. The sweetest and smallest French chocolate shop, fanciful half moons and whimsical décor hanging in the big windows. The strongest scent of sugar drifted down the lovely little lane from the gelato shop at the top of the walkway. Daniel said, "It looks like a street in Venice, Italy!" We found a modern restaurant with a cozy patio just upwind of the gelato shop's sugary sweetness and a few feet across from the chocolate shop. Sparkly, twinkly, and sugary. Perfect.

Our first real "fancy dinner date" together that week, we sat and shared a skinny flute of champagne. He ordered a roast chicken; I ate salmon with a buttery sauce. It felt like some kind of a dream or a scene from a ridiculously romantic movie. Dreamy and fancy and oh so *right* to be sitting there, gazing into his beautiful eyes, watching his nose wrinkle when he laughed. How he sat back, arms folded, and just stared at me.

Laughing, he led me down the street after dinner, peeking in shop windows and ducking in boutiques. Darkness covered Laguna Beach but we could hear the waves crashing out at sea. Holding hands was so new and exciting, my whole body felt electrified whenever his arm brushed up against mine.

He led me by the hand into an art shop. The walls were covered with eclectic paintings and inventive pieces of art. We walked through the entire shop, up the stairs and underground.

Daniel's eyes sparkled. He noticed a display of necklaces on the counter and touched them, looking at me. Seeing his wide, anticipating eyes, I exclaimed, "Oh these necklaces are so cute!"

Little tiny glass bottles were filled with glittery sand from Laguna, colored in different shades and hanging on a silver chain with a tag on it that read "Dream." He picked one up, gingerly, his tan, rough construction working/viola playing-hands looking so manly holding the delicate piece of jewelry. He chose the one filled with pink glitter.

I smiled.

He knows me already, I thought.

$36.99 was paid and he opened the fastener. Right there in the art shop, he lifted up my hair and circled the silver chain around my neck, clasping it.

He turned me around, looking into my eyes and said, "This is a token. A reminder. A promise. So you know: I am coming back to California."

This was a man I knew I could trust.

Terminal Three

We drove two and a half hours back to my family's

home that night and by the time we arrived, it was well after 1:00 AM. Daniel's flight the next morning left at 8:00AM. But we didn't care. We couldn't bear to say "goodnight." We stayed up all night talking in the living room, sitting side by side on the couch. Midway through the night, I leaned up beside him and laid my head on his shoulder as we held hands.

We talked of the week, and how it was the most perfect, beautiful whirlwind.

That week felt something like four sensational episodes of "The Bachelor" — complete with the epic traveling, beautiful scenery and gorgeous painted sunsets but happily lacking the drama, catfights, kissing, and cocktail parties.

Seven days together. And now, this cowboy would board a jet and fly half way across the country to his home in Oklahoma. As of that moment, we had no plans to see one another again.

It was a scary yet exciting place to be.

"I'll drive my truck out here. I'm coming back in March…to Santa Barbara with my family. We will see each other then, all the time! But…that is so so far away."

Tears threatened to spill from my eyes.

More than a month apart.

"What if you come to Oklahoma? Just come! To the farm, meet the family! They'd love it. We could be crazy and drive out to California in my truck, together!"

"Yes!! Yes! I'll do it!"

Heads full of dreams and hearts full of love, just beginning to bloom and blossom.

At 5:00 AM, we left the house and drove to LAX, before traffic hit. I held onto his arm, the entire drive. LAX is not close to my family's home, by any means. Every other drive there seems to have taken a century. But this time? Getting-closer-to-the-airport landmarks flew past the window. No traffic to speak of. And I hung onto his arm, my head on his shoulder, soaking in every last second.

Not knowing – for sure – when I would see him again.

All the way down the 5 freeway, I held onto him tightly. He kept saying his stomach hurt. "I'm just so upset to leave you."

I reached over and held onto his waist, my head in the crook of his neck.

How were we ever apart?

That week, every time we got in the car, the same few country songs had played on the radio, over and over and over. I'll never forget the peace and pure happiness of leaning all the way over the console, my arms around his waist and my chin up against the crook of his neck.

We parked. Unbuckling our seat belts and holding each other's faces. We didn't kiss. Not yet. It wasn't time. Wet tears ran down our faces – we were saying goodbye, too soon. It didn't feel right. Just days ago this boy waltzed into my life and now? I didn't ever want him to leave. How could I live without him?

We walked to Terminal 3, back to the place we met, just a week before.

He stopped, holding onto his belly.

Turning around and racing toward the nearest trash can, he leaned over it, his backpack strapped on, his light ripped jeans held up by a leather belt. I grabbed onto his suitcase, left by the door, and rolled it over to him. He dry-heaved into the airport trash can. I patted his back and nervous-laughed. It was all so hilarious and quick, wonderful and crazy. As he hung his head over the round trash lid, he muttered sheepishly, "I'm sorry you had to see that."

"I just can't bear the thought of leaving you." He moaned. So much, it made him sick.

I know, I whispered.

Just seven days. That's all it took.

Sometimes, you just *know.*

It was different than ever before.

Hot tears streamed down my cheeks. We hugged, his big arms encircling me, for a long time.

And then, he went.

I stood, watching him ride up the escalator. Blowing kisses and wiping tears.

He was gone. I placed my hand over my mouth as I cried hard for a few minutes. Tears of happiness, uncertainty, relief, joy, – wondering…when (and would) I ever embrace him again? Exhaustion from lack of sleep plus being sick that week hit me like a train.

We texted and called back and forth the next few days. It was as if we'd never not been in one another's lives.

When he arrived back home in Oklahoma, his mom texted me: "He misses you. And he has a 'glow.'"

He sent me a selfie with little Mercy. He said, "God made the week together perfect for us :) Every little thing!!"

One week together – one month apart.

He called me "Princess" all the time. And I called him "Cowboy."

We texted all day, and talked on the phone every night until the wee hours of the morning. I felt bad because he got up early for work, but he said he didn't mind. It was worth it to talk to me.

On February 27th, he woke me up at 5:00 AM with a text:

"Good morning Special Girl :) hope your day is the best! Miss you lots!"

Attached, he sent a photo of himself in his truck, pointing down to the middle seat. "The middle seat is calling your name little girl :) want you right beside me!!!" During "the week" he told me that was partly why he bought that truck: because he'd always imagined "his girl" sitting right beside him. On one of our late night calls, he told me, "I want you right up there in the middle seat right beside me." With the thickest put-on southern cowboy accent I'd ever heard. He made me laugh harder than anybody.

Red Dirt Roads

> *"It is astonishing how short a time it takes*
> *for very wonderful things to happen."*
> Frances Hodgen Burnet

Soon, I booked a one-way flight to Oklahoma City. I would be road tripping back to California with my cowboy. When my dad heard, he insisted we think ahead and make plans to stay with family or friends along the way. It was a seventeen hour trip! Daniel and I talked and made plans to stay with his cousin one night and his aunt's home the next.

I wondered, would we become "official" soon? Officially boyfriend and girlfriend?

I'll never forget flying over the patchwork fields of the Midwest, landing in OKC. I prayed, asking the Lord to guide and direct our time. My heart pounded wildly as I turned the corner to meet him. I reached my hand up to hold onto my "Laguna" necklace…I'd worn it every day since we'd parted.

This is it, I thought. Reunited. Finally!

Sandy, longer hair and sparking blue eyes. There he was, standing at the end, waiting for me.

Just for me. His girl.

 I ran toward him, jumping into his open arms!

A thousand butterflies in my stomach.

And all was right with the world.

We drove to the farm, sitting side by side in the truck

cab. I, in his middle seat, just like he'd always imagined. I met his big family, overwhelmed at remembering their names. They were so kind and sweet.

I slept in the girl's room. Two bunks beds and four girls in one small room. Seven boys down the hall in the big bedroom?

Wait, is this "The Walton's"?

The next morning, we woke up on the farm – the warm family, green grass, big fields, and red barn – my country girl heart, enchanted with Oklahoma. I wore a chambray dress with a sweetheart neckline and leather boots. Daniel showed me around all his old haunts with the little kids. The back pasture, the pond, everything.

"Let's go to my land. I want to show you." He said, taking my hand.

We got in the truck and drove down dusty dirt roads listening to country music and beaming. I loved seeing him in his element, where he'd grown up. When we rounded a corner and drove up his dirt driveway, lined in trees and brush – his land – I felt I understood him, just a little bit more. We parked the truck on the driveway. It was too overgrown to drive, so we walked. Hand in hand.

And then, in the distance, I saw it – his house! I

gasped.

"Oh, it is beautiful…" I said, squeezing his hand, tears threatening to spill. Somehow, it just hit me as I stood there on that land, looking up at that house up the road in the little cozy cove.

A piece of *him*.

This beautiful boy and all his hard work and visions.

Who he was: that farm boy with his head full of dreams, saving every dollar, denying himself so much, to make an investment in his future and prayed-for wife and family.

And who he became these past years. Disappointment and depression settling in on his soul. Moving to the East Coast, leaving the land sitting idle while weeds overgrew it and red dust covered the white walls. Half-used building material, a hammer, a bunch of nails in a weathered looking box, just lying in there. Abandoned in the midst of the last project. I could almost feel the longing and toil of how much he wanted and worked for it. And I could feel the ache of things that had come after.

We walked into the house, with tall windows beside the door, a huge chimney on the right side, all framed and ready. In his mind, he knew exactly where everything "was."

"The bedroom over here, with a big tub and closet and bathroom. The stairs here. The kitchen here with an island. A huge fireplace over here between these two windows…."

I loved that he was sharing his old dream with me. It made me feel very honored and special.

We spent a while looking at the house and walking the land. Then, when we walked back to the truck, he took me in his arms and said, "We should have a picnic!"

I smiled.

"How fun, we should! Let's plan it sometime!"

With a twinkle in his eye, he opened up the cab. All in one sweeping moment, he took out a wicker picnic basket covered by a bright pink gingham cloth, his guitar, a vase of wildflowers, and his grandmother's pink quilt.

Stunned. He'd planned this?

"How 'bout we have our picnic *now*?" His eyes danced and nose wrinkled as he laughed and smiled at my shock. I jumped up and down and wrapped my arms around his neck.

He told me about an old schoolhouse situated back from his house. I swooned. I love the "olden days."

We carried our picnic things past his house and through a field, ducking under a barbed wire fence toward one room schoolhouse, painted white with green trim. "Ah!" I exclaimed. "I love it! It's so 'Little House on the Prairie'! I can't get over it!"

Under a grouping of trees, he spread the quilt on the dried grass and leaves. Unexpectedly warm for March, the sun shone bright on us all afternoon. He set the blue glass Mason jar full of pink and yellow wildflowers in the center, the picnic basket beside it, his guitar on the edge.

It was a very special and very thoughtful picnic. He remembered all my favorite things: a little box of chocolate, Voss water, a delicious sandwich and chips, fruit, and pink champagne.

We ate, and sipped and laughed. It was a magical afternoon, just the two of us on that quilt, no one in the world but us.

Finishing our little meal with creamy chocolates, Daniel stood up and reached his hand down to me. He smiled and said, "Come on! Let's play a game in the school yard like the school kid who used to share their lunch and play here years and years ago!" And he took off running. We ran around that cozy little school house just like I imagined they did a hundred years ago, playing tag and laughing 'til our sides ached. He chased me as I screamed, playfully catching me and stopping me, his arms on my shoulders. Breathless, he stopped.

"I have a question for you…"

My heart skipped a beat.

"I have *the* biggest crush on you. Will you be my girlfriend?"

"Yes yes yes!" I cried. Such perfect happiness! He spun me around in circles as we laughed with sheer joy.

It was one of the happiest moments of my whole life. I felt like flying!

Little butterflies flitted around us, the first ones of the year. He sat me down on the quilt again and told me he had a special surprise. He told me he wrote a song, a few years ago, for "my girl."

Taking his guitar out of its case, he began to strum and sing.

"Sometimes, I thought I'd found you, but God said no…."

The song he wrote for his future wife on the Empire State Building. "Praying For You." For me!

Oh, the happiness! I could not contain it.

Walking back to the truck, picnic basket on my arm, we found our way back to his house. We chatted and giggled, happily buzzing around, in the thick of love.

Spontaneously, we began to dance. In the house with no roof, birds chirping and sun setting. I'd never felt so happy.

He spun me around and then I'd twirl back into him. Over and over. I reached up and encircled my arms around his neck, just gazing into his eyes. He nuzzled his nose against mine. Back and forth, back and forth. In that moment, I just knew I wanted to kiss him. And he wanted to kiss me.

We'd never once spoken of kissing. But, somehow, we just knew. This was it.

His soft lips brushed mine and we kissed.

Oh, the kiss!

The most wonderful kiss any two people have ever had. We stepped back, elated.

And I made the face Taylor Swift makes when she wins an award.

Ahhhhh!

I jumped up and down, screaming.

"That was my *first kiss*!"

Smiling and spinning around, he exclaimed, "What?! It was mine too!"

We danced and twirled and jumped up and down.

Happiness itself!

This wonderful Oklahoma cowboy who stole my heart? I gave him my first kiss. And he gave me his.

It was magical and perfect, beautiful and pure. Good and so right. Long awaited and blessed.

I felt like he was most likely my future husband. But, of course, we didn't know "for sure." Only God knew. Yet, I kissed him – not because I just got caught up in a moment or because I just couldn't wait any longer. Not because I was 100% sure he was "the one." We barely knew each other, and I did not know for sure if we would marry someday.

Yet, I knew this man well enough to know he was a man of integrity and character. A man who valued women and treated me with the utmost respect. A man who had kept and saved himself physically for his future wife and understood my desire and passion to do the same for my future husband. We'd both said "no" to kissing (and everything else) with others before.

But we just knew. Together. Our hearts, matching, our pages, the same. We knew that the person we just gave our first kiss to honored it, respected it, cherished it, and fully understood its value. And we knew, it wouldn't be something used as a step toward other things too soon.

Just a kiss.

The most magical kiss in the world.

When we arrived back at the farm, we were showered with congratulations and little gifts from the girls of the family. Mercy handed me a little yellow flower she picked on the farm. Of course, I still have it today.

An Oklahoma Love Story

Noah: "You wanna dance with me?"
Allie: "Sure. Now?"
Noah: "Mmm Hmm"
Allie: "You're not supposed to dance in the street."
Noah: "You are supposed to dance in the street."
Allie: "Yeah, but we don't have any music."
Noah: "Well, we'll make some... Bum bum bum bum bum bum..."
Allie: "You're a terrible singer."
Noah: "I know."
Allie: "And I like this song."
The Notebook

Our budding romance was a long-awaited, happy whirlwind and I was on my way to being very well swept off my feet. The night after he asked me to be his girl, we went on a dinner date in Oklahoma City. As the evening came to a close, he drove his black pickup truck to the middle of his small, sleepy town - not to the farm as I expected.

He parked his black ford in a spot in front of Rick's Coffee Shop and jumped out. He ran around to my side of the truck and opened the door, leading me out into the street by my hand.

He asked: "You wanna dance with me?" and swept me off my feet as we waltzed on Oklahoma avenue.

My eyes darted around. We were in the street. The middle of the street! Just like Allie and Noah...in one of my favorite love stories.

Taking me tenderly in his arms, we slowed danced on the black asphalt. Everything felt totally still and peaceful. Life was perfect in that moment, perfectly good.

And this man? I was falling for him.

He laid down on the black asphalt and I laid by him, watching the street light turn.

Green, yellow, red.

Green, yellow, red.

Talking of dreams and hopes and everything and nothing at all.

Until a car's headlights flashed in front of us and a horn honked wildly as we jumped up, screaming and laughing while it flew past.

I liked that song.

This whole new falling in love (and kissing) thing really was wonderful. And it was all really rather innocent. Once back in the truck, we kissed as we sat, just staring into one another's eyes, totally mesmerized and falling very quickly head over heels in love. Probably for a good ten minutes.

One day in, and kissing was a peck on the lips and it was *absolute magic.*

Out of the corner of my eye, I noticed something moving out the front glass windshield. My door was locked and I leaned up on it, but Daniel's was open still.

I turned my head and suddenly saw a man wearing a huge brown horse head! He stood in front of the truck, close to the windshield, staring in the window by Daniel's open door. He held a cigarette up to his mouth, a trail of smoke snaking upward above his jet black mane.

He stood, unmoving, watching us silently.

I looked up and I gasped and screamed. I literally almost passed out.

The street was totally desolate, as small towns tend to be at midnight.

Daniel looked up and jumped.

Slamming his door and locking it, quickly putting the truck in reverse, he let out the first and last real curse word I've ever heard him utter.

My heart raced as we *tore* out of the parking space, racing down the road.

"Oh my goodness, *that was so creepy!*" I said, shaking and panting.

"Are you okay?!" He asked. I nodded.

He fiddled with the radio as we drove out of Guthrie, hearts racing. "We need some worship music." He said, breathing fast.

A worship song struggled through the static on the radio.

He drove. Then, he began to pray with authority and boldness and faith.

For protection and peace. For whatever demonic agenda that tried to steal from our special date and scare us to be shut down. That the Lord would be the center of our relationship, the focus. That we would honor Him in all we did together. That He would lead and guide us.

He prayed, fervently. All the way back to the farm.

I sat, in awe.... This kind of man really exists? A man of faith? A man whose first and automatic response in an unexpected moment of fear or negativity or attack from the enemy is to raise his hands and bow his head, seeking Jesus?

Safely back at the farm, Daniel held me close and told me that we needed to let that unsettling incident go. That we needed to focus on all the good things the Lord accomplished that day, and how special our date and our "Notebook" moment was.

I smiled and sighed, happy that it happened, really, because the Lord showed me more of Daniel's strong character and godly heart through it.

He was more than just a good looking, talented man.

He was a real man of God.

I felt very thankful to see His heart and character in action.

This is the kind of man I want to marry.

Slow Dancing in the Rain

We explored Guthrie the next morning. The day looked cloudy and the sky, heavy. Rain would most likely be falling, sometime soon. He walked me around the little shops and streets. I became enchanted with the small old town and especially it's charmingly perfect Victorian houses.

 We walked to the edge of town, past the railroad station and into the old silos. I'd never been in a silo before. The walls covered in graffiti, we posed for photos and talked and teased and flirted.

Somehow, we ended up slow dancing again (to no music) a theme in our early days…being so enchanted and in love just called for spontaneous slow dancing, I suppose.

I gently began to sing a favorite song in his ear. My voice echoed in the silo, making it sound big.

"Someday, when I'm awfully low
When the world is cold
I will feel a glow just thinking of you…and the way you look tonight."

His eyes, wide and enthralled.

Little did we know, we'd dance again one year later to

that very same song…our first dance as husband and wife.

Next, we broke into a worship song. Singing in harmony, his voice low and mine high. We just fit.

Like two puzzle pieces, like a hand in a glove, like salt and pepper – matching hearts, in every sense.

We were two of a kind, and falling very quickly into a romance from which we would never recover.

The local Pollard Theater showed a performance of Helen Keller that evening and he took me. It felt very old-fashioned in the most romantic sense – going to a cozy old theater to a real life play instead an impersonal $12 movie in the middle of a big, concrete jungle city. A hundred twinkle lights danced all over the theater and down the quint Guthrie streets. When we made our way back to the truck in the parking lot, the velvety black sky opened up and, rained. We ducked into the truck for cover, slamming our doors shut. His eyes twinkled as he looked at me, mischievously. That look I began to know (and now know very well) when he gets a kind of "crazy" and usually very wild and free idea and throws it out, not knowing how I'll respond. "Wanna kiss me in the rain, baby?"

"Umm, heck yeah!"

We leapt out of the truck, warm rain falling and

soaking our hair. He pushed me up against the truck and kissed me for a minute, thoroughly (Rhett Butler would've been very proud of him.) Rain drops falling, twinkle lights sparkling all around.

My boots in a puddle and I didn't care.

Even today, it stands as the single most romantic moment of my life.

Though it may sound a little silly, my starry-eyed Anne of Green Gables sort of heart prayed, as a young girl, that someday, I could be kissed – really kissed – by a good and wonderful man – in the rain.

Another wish, another prayer: come true.

My last day in Oklahoma, he took me back to his land as night fell. I'd told him how much I love roasting marshmallows and making s'mores. So, he searched for graham crackers, chocolates, and marshmallows in the farm pantry. He found a couple of metal sticks to roast them on, and we drove up the dusty red roads to his land.

Wearing rugged cowboy work boots and ripped light jeans, a soft white sweater, his messy hair framing his perfect face.

His blue eyes pierced mine whenever he looked at me. And did something to my soul.

The darkness around us felt comforting and the black sky above us hung, like velvet.

He started a fire with his bare hands and a couple of sticks.

And I said, "Um....you *are* a real-life cowboy. They don't make those in California!"

Sitting on a log by the fire, we warmed our hands and roasted our marshmallows. The stars twinkled above in the night sky.

All was right with the world.

The Road Trip

Daniel packed up his truck with all his things, ready to take off to California – for at least the month of March, maybe longer.

Never in my life will I forget the thrill of that trip. We hopped into his old black pickup truck and took off on the adventure of a lifetime. An adventure we didn't know then, would never end.

As we waved goodbye to the Morris family, he handed me a little brown box tied in pink and white baker's twine. Folded into a little tissue paper was a thin and tiny white and pink beaded bracelet. He'd picked it out, himself.

"I wanted to give you a little gift to start our road trip."

I wiped away tears, overwhelmed by the thoughtfulness of this young man I now got to call "boyfriend."

We drove through Kansas, right through the town where my only boyfriend before Daniel had lived. Seeing it "in person" was a full-circle moment for me. I wouldn't have fit there, with him. I fit right here, in this middle seat next to Daniel.

We stayed two nights in Colorado with his kind cousin, wife, and little boys and with his quirky might-as-well-be aunt and her family. Snow fell like baby powder our first day. I relished being in a new place, the air thin and crisp and cold. Out of the Rocky Mountains of Colorado, we stopped at a Chili's in very hot Utah. The weather felt blistery hot, different from the cold Colorado Rockies we'd just driven through early that morning — snow on their tops and all.

On the road for a good twelve hours already we kept powering through and somehow we stayed awake. We ran out of people to stay with, so we had to just keep going.

Oklahoma to Kansas to Colorado to Utah to Nevada to California.

As the sun set over the wide desert, we stopped at Starbucks right outside Las Vegas.

Back on the road, we sipped iced chai tea lattes and laughed until our sides ached. To keep ourselves awake, we rolled down the windows and asked each other questions. I found a list of one hundred questions to ask on a first date. "Who was your first crush?" and "What is your dream vacation?" And "What's your most embarrassing moment?"

We were the kind of tired that makes you almost hysterical.

Exhausted to the core, but somehow we stayed awake; the pitter-pattering of my heart and the pace at which I fell for this wild, quiet, beautiful, blue eyed man made me race with adrenaline.

I've never felt very comfortable around boys, having no brothers and just a few guy friends in my whole life. But Daniel? He suddenly felt like a best friend.

We now look back on that wild and free road trip, wondering *how on earth* we did not get in a car accident somewhere along a lonely stretch of desert highway.

It really wasn't that safe, 'cause let's face it: we basically just sat in the car, gazing into each other's eyes all those long hours. I intermittingly leaned over his seat and gave him pecks on the cheek or lips as he tried his best to keep his poor eyes on the road and hands on the wheel. (Don't try that at home, kids!)

We arrived in California at my family's mountain home, almost twenty hours later. It was the most exhilarating and exhausting trip of my life.

Yet, I felt like I knew this cowboy a lot better. And I liked him, even more.

Santa Barbara Sea Breeze

Farmer's markets and coffee shops, white washed buildings and enchanting beaches. A place I grew up visiting. I remember my grandma Dot always talked about how dreamy Santa Barbara is, and how she wished she could live there. Daniel and his twin, his wife and their baby set up camp for the month in a little old house on Chapala Street. For most of the days they spent there, I gratefully crashed with them. As a little girl, when imagining my future romance, I always pictured it to be neat and tidy — oh, it would be passionate, but it would fall into nice, clean lines. I'd have perfect self-control and flawless discernment. I would keep my friendships with my girls up and never be "one of those" who because all googly-eyed and distracted by a boy. I'd communicate with my future husband well and be an open book. Not sharing too much and never holding too much back. But, in real life? I became completely swept into the dating-Daniel-whirlwind. I didn't call people back or reply to emails, my family adored Daniel but kind of felt like I went MIA. I pretty much let my blog go for a long while. I learned that real life isn't always what we expect or plan.

That month was filled with beachside fun and frolic, two love birds, eyes glossed over and distracted, to the fullest extent of the word. We were hard to get ahold of, let alone make plans with and always late because we just couldn't quite keep track of time like we used to.

We talked about physical boundaries in our relationship. And set them. Not because certain things were "bad" or we would not be blessed if we did them. Daniel told me, one evening as we ate spoonsful of McConnell's ice cream, that he saw sexual and physical boundaries in a relationship less as restrictions and "no no's because if you do ___, God will be angry." No... he saw it instead as keeping certain things special and sacred for marriage.

Not because "if we do A, B, and C God will bless us." But because, He says certain things are best saved for marriage and we want the safest, most joyful marriage and life together possible! We weren't "perfect" in holding our boundaries throughout our relationship. There were times when we'd push a little too far, and then take a step back and reevaluate where we were. Our end-goal and hearts were the same, though. Girls often ask me how to maintain physical boundaries in a romantic relationship. My #1 advice is: the man you're dating *absolutely must* hold the same values as you do in treating sex and physical romance as sacred, meant for marriage, and putting the other person first is key. If not, you're fighting a losing battle.

Dating someone is a crash course in learning about their character, and Daniel proved to be a man of extremely honorable character. I was absolutely blown away. There were times in our relationship when we crossed a little over certain boundaries we chose to set at certain seasons….and *he* was the one who would say, "Let's take a step back." I can truly and honestly say that he is the strongest man I know and this is another reason I knew he was the kind of man I wanted to marry.

Looking back, we count those Santa Barbara days as the sweet time we fell in love.

Won't You Be My Sweetheart?

On May 2nd, we spent the day with Daniel's family at Disneyland. It was Daniel's first time!

We went on as many rides as we could, eating good food, and just enjoying each other and the happy atmosphere.

I remember being exhausted that night after watching the fireworks. He and I sat, side by side on the little cut out benches of that drawbridge in front of the sparkling, grand, lit up castle.

Laying my head on his shoulder, I drifted in and out

of falling asleep. He kept talking. Sort of nervously. Barely trailing onto what he was saying, my eyes darted open when I heard him say three little words that changed my life forever.

"Baby....I love you."

And right that second, *"Won't you be my sweetheart? I'm in love with you"* played softly over magical hidden speakers.

It was my beloved great grandparent's love song!

It was magic. Rare magic. The kind you can't hold onto, that's like sparkly fairy dust floating above your head.

"I love you too!" I said, and wrapped my arms around his neck.

The park was ours that night, *our* land, to revel in being *in love*. For real! Really! No more "he loves me; he loves me not" wondering or questions. Just basking in the hope, happiness and joy of it all.

He held onto my hand tightly as we ran out of the park when it closed, and hopped on the shuttle, planning to meet his family who'd left earlier. We were sitting high, riding on Cloud 9. It felt smooth as silk and sweet as pie.

My insides were like the inside of a bag of popcorn in

the microwave, and my head was spinning with happiness.

He loved me.

I loved him!

It was real and it felt so long-awaited. And really, really good.

Suddenly, Daniel's phone rang. It was Caleb. He explained that the family was at the local hospital. There had been an emergency.

We immediately put the address into our GPS and drove into the night. We quickly parked in a big, gray cement parking garage that smelled like exhaust, I coughed. Daniel gave me his sweater as we darted across the cold, echoing structure, into an elevator. A dark haired, middle aged woman held the elevator door open for us as we rushed to make it in time. She held a paper coffee cup in one hand and an overnight bag in the other.

Daniel sighed heavily.

"I hate hospitals." He whispered.

"Because of Joel?" I asked, softly.

"Mmmhmm."

He looked at me.

It felt like going from one world to a different one.

Drastically different. It was like a scene in a movie —
when the director calls "cut" and one bright happy
scene is completely shifted and the screen is taken
over by some dark, very different setting. The slap in
the face that also slaps the popcorn out of your hands
and Mickey Mouse ears off your head and lands you
in a dark, cold, rather scary world, instead.

A dark haired lady smiled at me.

Ding. The door slid open, harshly.

We followed her out of the big metal elevator and into
a huge white, very brightly lit hallway. Teddy bears
and toys looked at us through a window, a gift shop.
Primary colors filled a bulletin board on one wall.
There was not a soul in sight, and it seemed very
open, very empty, very clean, very white, and very
stark.

"Where is emergency?!" Daniel asked, frustrated. I'd
never seen him upset before. Or scared. Or sad.
Because, really? We had just met, and the time we had
spent together was full of literal rainbows, cups of
steamy sweet drinks, stomach butterflies, flirty glances,
flowers, seaside adventures, and birds singing.

"This is sick. We need to find them." Daniel tried his

phone, to call his twin. But, no service.

The dark-haired lady had made her way far along down the big bright white open hallway, but she turned all the way around and began walking quickly back toward me and Daniel. She must have heard his frustrated comment.

Smiling, she asked, "Are you looking for the ER? That is in the hospital across the street, actually!" She gave us directions on how to get there, and continued: "This is the *children's* hospital, and this here is the floor for kids with terminal illnesses. This happens to a lot of people! So no worries, it *is* confusing!" she said, sweetly.

"But I know, because I'm here a lot! My son is in this ward, actually." She said it cheerily, somehow. There was something brave about her that I didn't think I've ever seen before in a person.

As we walked away, Daniel's face fell.

I thought of Joel.

And how just a mere few years ago, Daniel's mama was that woman. How his family spent every day, waking up and packing up and going to the children's cancer ward of the hospital in their nearest city. How they would pack overnight bags and bring coffee cups and sit and pray their hearts out and cry their guts out. In the midst of all the joy we were walking through, I was reminded of the pain in our stories, the paths that led us here with broken roads, loss, and darkness. It somehow gave me a greater, more vivid picture of the things Daniel had seen and known. Things I have never tasted. Like death of a sibling, a dear little toddler… far too young to say goodbye to life here on this earth. A baby with so many years ahead, with promise as big as the sky.

We rushed into the Emergency Room, our eyes darting to the right and to the left.

The lights were bright and the walls were stark. The fairy dust was long gone. Popcorn and sugar didn't waft through the air, it was replaced by the smell of fake plastic and strong disinfectant. Whimsical, happy songs didn't play merrily around us… they were replaced by the sound of random, harsh "beeeeeps," feet slapping quickly on the linoleum floors, steel metal doors slamming.

We sat with Daniel's little nephew in the waiting room. Every ten minutes, an alarm would go off, glaringly and blaring. They would jump in their sleep, and then settle back into the chair. My eyes were plastered open all night.

We left the hospital at 9AM. Daniel got on a plane for Maryland the next morning. He would spend many weeks that summer and early autumn flying back and forth from DC to LA. He'd just transplanted his whole life to a foreign city and still had responsibilities and commitments to fulfill in Maryland. He'd signed contracts and been paid money to play viola at weddings, months before.

We kissed goodbye for the week.

A June Apart

"No one tells you how hard it is. Falling in love."
"Sarah, Plain and Tall."

At the end of May, he would again leave for Maryland and spend a month performing at weddings.

A month apart.

Daunting and unwelcome.

We spent an afternoon sipping tea and wandering rose gardens at The Huntington Library. He treated me to all my favorite things. "Thank you for sitting here in a fancy tea room with me." I said, grateful a big strong guy would unashamedly eat tiny finger sandwiches and drink tea from a porcelain cup. He winked. "You're my girl, and I'm the luckiest man in the world to be sitting here with you."

The next morning, I drove him to LAX. Stuck in the horrible 405 traffic for far longer than we anticipated, we ran to the terminal, late.

He missed his flight!

And we could do nothing but buy another expensive ticket for later that afternoon.

I felt so sorry for him at the turn of events. But, I am lying if I say I wasn't a wee bit happy to steal a few more hours with my love.

To pass the time, we caught a movie, got some coffee, and then dinner.

Outside, it began to rain. Aptly.

I sat close to him. I couldn't even finish my salad. How could I bear to live life without him for a whole month? It truly felt like an eternity was ahead of us.

With rain, falling softly on our heads, we walked to his truck, preparing to drive back to the airport. I held his arm and tears streamed down my face, mixing with the rain.

Lord, I can't do this.

Daniel stopped and took my face in his hands. "Baby, maybe the Lord has a plan for us to spend these weeks apart. Maybe it's the best thing and will help us grow closer to Him and to each other." He prayed, right there on the sidewalk, that the Lord would lead and guide us, and the time apart would be fruitful and wouldn't feel too long.

Amen.

I raised my head and lo and behold, up in the sky right in front of us: a perfect, full rainbow!

Be still and trust in my promises. The Lord spoke to my heart.

Peace washed over me with the rain that fell.

We said goodbye, and prepared our hearts for a month apart.

Many phone calls filled our evenings. Late into the night, we talked. But something was missing. There were things we'd never talked about, parts of our hearts and stories, never shared. We both knew it was time to share them.

Two weeks into our time separated that June, he called me – much later than we planned, his voice, shaky on the other line. The last few hours, he'd spent with his Maryland family, talking. They told him they could see that he and I were not talking about some important things. That we were not opening up as fully as we could and in order for our relationship to move forward, we needed to get "down and dirty" in our conversations. To truly, with open hands, be honest about some very important topics. And to not fear it.

Because, in all honesty, we were both scared. Half to

death.

He went out to his car that night and sat until early in the morning, talking to me on the phone. Caleb remembers seeing him out the window when he went to bed and again when he woke up.

He said to me, "There are things we are afraid of talking about. And we really need to just talk about them." And so, we started. Just like that. And all night long, we talked and talked and talked. We opened up, in honesty.

It felt awkward and imperfect, new and scary.

It felt like letting go. Letting go of fear and walking into the unknown, which, really, is freedom.

We had been scared to mess it up, ruin the magic, steal the joy or rock the boat. Our love story so far: unearthly, incandescent happiness. The happiest we'd ever been!

Bringing up pain or struggles, imperfections or difficult topics, well, we didn't want to dampen the fairy dust! We didn't want to screw it up.

It made him want to run. It made me want to hide.

Yet, when the flower of communication and honesty was pulled open, it wasn't painful, really. It was freeing.

We realized, then and there, that night, *the root of the magic would be honesty and openness*. Dating for a purpose, as we were, considering the real possibility of marriage in the future – it needed to be.

From that day forward, we walked into a new freedom together. It felt so good to be totally real, and not be afraid to bring up hard things – completely open, unashamed, and unafraid.

Many deep, important, life-bringing, conversation-prompting and relationship-altering discussions came out of it for us. Asking and answering, opening up and sharing. Telling stories and secrets, raw tears and belly laughter, and being very real, vulnerable, and open. Talk of marriage and future plans was often a topic of conversation. It happened over time through our relationship.

We were reunited in July and oh so happy! He met me at the airport once again, wearing navy shorts, Sperry's, a white shirt, and holding a bouquet of lovely pink and yellow flowers in his hand.

Someday Is Today

The summer wore on. Though seasons don't change much in Southern California, autumn began to peer its head around the corner.

We both knew… the desire for "the future" shared – on our hearts, bloomed softly… over time. We processed and felt – I want you, only you – forever. This is meant to be. We talked about it, often. Throughout the warm days of summer, I would jokingly point at my left ring finger in moments of discussing the future, widening my eyes and tilting my head teasingly, without saying a word. He'd laugh. "I'm workin' on it!" I jokingly (or not so jokingly) sent him photos of dream rings.

Wild and freely pursuing adventures, dreams, and goals, we talked of children and family, home and lifestyle, expectations and convictions. We talked of wedding dress styles, venues, and timelines.

Mandy often asked me: "Now, what is your *ideal* ring? This one? That one? This cut, this size?"

It was coming, I knew. I just didn't know when. Until, he began hinting around in mid-August. He told me, "So….I want to recreate our first week." My wheels began turning, right off, especially when he chose the second week of September and asked me to set it aside. He said we would go to all our special places.

When a friend invited us over for dinner that week, he quickly jumped in: "Oh no! We have a plan that week." I knew something was up. Mom and Mandy heard my suspicions. "So…Daniel keeps saying we are going to 'recreate our first week' What if he proposes? I feel like he might…!"

Realizing my always-noticing mind was racing with

guesses, he "threw me off the scent" with some carefully-crafted, good-hearted little white lies.

During the summertime, he went to a bridal show as a vendor. While there (unbeknownst to me) a jeweler approached him, handing him a card and asking him to play some music at an event they were hosting for brides the next day. He played for their event. They fell in love with his music, and that day – the search for *the* ring began. The jeweler graciously offered him a special deal. Of course, I was blind to it all, yet he feared I would catch on. He sweetly covered all his tracks, wanting me to be totally surprised.

He and my parents – and especially wonderful Mandy, crafted an elaborate plan for the proposal. I now know that she snuck down to the ring shop with him a few times.
A plan was in the works. And Daniel came up with a good one! One I could not have ever guessed! On September 9, I got a random email from a sweet blog friend and stylist, Jackie Rose Fitzgerald. She wrote that she would love for me to come to Laguna Beach on September 20th for a fashion photo shoot. We happily planned the shoot and I couldn't wait.

I didn't know that Dad said yes.

That Daniel chose a ring.

And made plans. Plans to create a magical, special, significant night of a lifetime, and that many of our people and family were "in" on it.

A life-altering question would be asked and an answer would be given, and that would change the course of our lives.

Daniel knew he wanted to propose at Laguna Beach.

As he planned and thought of ways to make the proposal happen there, he remembered I once told him about my internet friend, Jackie, and how she loved Laguna Beach too. And so, he searched my Facebook, looking through every friend on my friend's list, for a whole week until he found that stylist with blonde hair who matched my description. He then found her website, looked for her phone number, called her up and told her the plan, asking for her help.

In an effort to truly keep me in the dark and totally surprise me with the extravagant proposal, Daniel went to all ends and expended all effort to keep his secret.

In Maryland on a trip, he devised a little plan to make sure I would not guess anything and spoil the surprise.

One night while he was gone, Mandy and I decided to have a girl's night in a local hotel.

Daniel called to say goodnight. He sounded down, different. His voice cracked as he told me, *"Babe, I have some bad news…*" and explained that while at Caleb's home, he got an unexpected letter in the mail from the IRS – he was unknowingly in some debt and so, he said, "I'm so sad. It means that 'certain things' will have to be postponed until sometime later…."

What?!

Knife to my heart.

I tried oh so hard to be encouraging and strong, letting him know it was okay.

We hung up, sad and dejected. I told Mandy over delivered pizza. She seemed shocked and sad.

I broke down and wept as I told mom and girlfriends over the phone that morning, eating pink donuts on the white hotel bedding.

Daniel came back to Los Angeles a few days later, and when I met him at Starbucks that evening, he seemed – and even looked - really sad.

My heart sank, disappointed that (clearly) our engagement would be delayed for who-knows-how-long. That week, we moved forward with life as usual and I did not expect a thing. I didn't ask too many questions about timelines, because – the poor guy was just trying to pay off debt and I did not want to pressure him or make him feel worse.

He said he still wanted to take a few days and recreate "our week," but I discouraged the plan, saying: *"Oh no, we don't need to do all that and spend all that money!"*

As the days went on, Jackie tagged me and Mandy in several of her Instagram photos, preparing outfits and J. Crew accessories for our photo shoot. I explained to Daniel that I was so excited to use the photos for the cover of my upcoming first print issue of my new dreamed-of magazine, Graceful.

The night before the shoot, Daniel called me to say goodnight. I invited him to come to the shoot with me, wanting him to see the process.

Disappointed, he told me that he had a gig come up – playing viola for an event in Malibu and would not be able to make it.

September 20th came, at last.

It was normal Saturday morning at home. Mom and Dad left the house early for a class (my dad is a college professor at a Christian seminary and Mom often helps him, especially with day-long Saturday courses.) They left early, and Mandy and I spent the morning at home – getting ready for our photoshoot that evening. I remember, when Dad and Mom shut the front door behind them, I turned to Mandy.

"Hmmm, that's odd. *Why* is Dad wearing *jeans* to class? He never, ever wears jeans to class..." She ignored me, texting someone on her phone.

If I had the power to hand one out, I'd give Mandy an Oscar for her performance the day of the engagement. She literally acted just as normal and "herself" as she always does. She had a major attitude about the photo shoot and I wondered if she would really come with me that evening. She did not seem anything but calm, normal, as if she could care less about the plan. She told me we needed to stop at her store at the mall (she managed a women's clothing boutique at the time) and she somehow got me to go into the shop to try on a white dress that she and her co-workers told me was *perfect* for a photo shoot at the beach that evening. Wanting to show up in something cute, I bought it.

Little did I know that she had already bought it in my size days before, held onto it in the back room, notified all her co-workers about the situation, and had it "staged" on the rack, ready for me to pick out on my own and "purchase" – she even coached her salesgirls to "fake sell it" to me. Little did I know that Daniel had come into the store earlier that week and picked it out for me to wear for the engagement.

While at the mall, I changed into the little white dress – but realized it was showing my bra in the back! Panic mode! We had just a few hours to get to Laguna Beach to meet Jackie's photographer at the Montage Hotel (the plan she emailed me) and we knew we'd most-likely encounter traffic. Mandy did not seem stressed about time, at *all*.

Leisurely, she sat at the nail salon, chatting with the stylists, deciding whether she would choose white or cream nail polish. I, always late but with an anxious eye on the clock, decided I didn't have time for a (much-needed) manicure.

Mandy insisted we had time (*"You're doing a photo shoot, Sis! And Jackie is really stylish. We need to have our nails done."*) So, I sat down, chose a cream polish and asked the nail technician to *"Please hurry, I'm so sorry but we have to be to Orange County in a few hours! And, traffic…."*

Looking back, it just felt like a normal day. But something about it felt different. Alive. Special. Even at that point. The sweet workers at the nail salon complimented me profusely, almost – looking back – as if they knew! *"You just look so gorgeous! Your dress, your hair!"* Before leaving the mall, I (with wet nails) ran down to Victoria's Secret and bought stylist's tape, hoping to secure my dress where it opened too far in the back.

We jumped in the car and braved LA traffic on the freeway. Mandy – calm as a cucumber all morning – suddenly seemed rattled. As we passed Disneyland, traffic became congested and almost stopped. We were an hour out from our destination, the iPhone told us. Just enough time. She blasted the rap music playing in her car (as usual) but started breathing more and more heavily as time went on.

I noticed she was texting someone, furiously.

I had no idea, of course – but, Daniel wondered where we were exactly – as he, Mom, Dad and our photographer were all working hard to craft and set-up the extravagant proposal, out on a rock in Laguna Beach.

He had it timed and planned perfectly. We would arrive just before sunset.

Mandy kept calm until a truck cut us off, causing us to nearly miss our (very important) exit – one that, had we missed it, would have taken more than half an hour to recover – and would, incidentally, have caused us to miss the proposal… all together. Of course, I knew none of this at the time. All I knew? Mandy flipped out. Now, we laugh at the scene – as her reaction is understandable. She had the most important scheduled date of my life so far, on her head.

At the time, though, I was a little shocked at the passion behind her road rage. She screamed and yelled at the semi-truck driver, rolling down the window and cussing a string of profanities – her eyes, wild, her fist beating the steering wheel – her hands honking the horn incessantly. I sat in the passenger's seat, shocked.

Quietly, I said, "Sis, wow…umm, calm down, okay? It's just a photo shoot, we can be a little late."

She rolled the window back up, panting. (This makes me smile now. She was responsible to get me to my once-in-a-lifetime engagement, and she would not let a single soul in the world stop her. Just a picture of our fierce sister-love, almost a "mama bear" kind of protective relationship we have with each other.)

Both of us have *the* smallest bladders in the history of the world, and so we just *had* to stop at a gas station bathroom right when we got off the freeway, near our destination.

We ran in. My open-back dress still a major wardrobe malfunction. The gas station mart did not sell sewing kits.

Time was ticking. The sun soon setting. I hoped Jackie might have a safety pin or something, as the stylist tape I'd purchased at the mall was not working. In desperation, I asked the gas station cashier if she had a safety pin or *something* on hand? She did. We pinned my dress. All was ready and well.

Behind the scenes, my precious parents had been working hard all day with my beautiful fiancé-to-be, to make our dream come true.

Arrive we did, barely on time and very out of breath. We almost missed the hotel, our GPS directed us to the wrong parking lot. Jackie had instructed us to drive up to the valet and meet her photographer and that she would be down on the beach, setting up props and preparing the shoot. We planned to follow her photographer down there and meet her, right as the sun was setting, to capture "golden hour" pictures.

Pulling up to the valet, we jumped out of the car (conscious of the rapidly setting sun) and began scanning the busy hotel front area for "the photographer." I spotted someone waving and walking quickly toward us. A smiling and bubbly young woman came bounding up – large camera strapped around her neck and held in one of her hands. Her other hand, reached out to shake mine. We hopped on the elevator, rushing down to the beach, following her through the lush hotel, past dark wood and the sound of clinking glass from the nearby hotel restaurant, down steps to the light-golden sand.

Suddenly, all became a whirlwind. I remember feeling cool sand on my toes as we ran toward the place Jackie supposedly waited.

The sun was setting very quickly in the pink sky around us, over the sea crystal blue – always clearer and cleaner and more "tropical" than any other California beach. I've always said, it reminds me so distinctly of my childhood trip to Greece – the water and foliage of Laguna looks very much like the Mediterranean Sea.

All of a sudden, Ally began snapping photos of me. She mentioned something like, "Oh I just want to get some shots of you girls walking up!" I mentioned something about, "Oh this is our place, Sis! The place Daniel played those songs for me that first week!"

And then – out of nowhere and faster than I could take it all in -I saw someone, so unexpectedly: *Daniel.*

Walking up toward me.

Through the beautiful arch.

He took me in his arms and kissed me.

Gasping and surprised, I asked, "What?! Baby! Wait. Why are you here? What are you doing here! You were supposed to be in Malibu! Ah, I am so glad you could come!!"

I remember how vividly his eyes sparkled.

He didn't say much. He just smiled.

At that moment, I thought he was simply surprising me at the photo shoot. So happy he could make it, but a little confused, too. It happened so fast and it seemed like such a big moment. I kept thinking, "Where's Jackie?"

And then, the world began spinning all at once. He took me by the hand, leading me through the arch.

I saw a long wooden sign with words painted, pink on white.

It read, "Someday is today."

I heard that very song, "Someday my Prince will come, someday I'll find my love...." playing loudly from a hidden speaker.

It hit me.

This is it.

My heart swelled. I shook. I gasped. My knees went weak.

> *"All this time, I believed with all I am*
> *that I would find you."*
> *Tyler Knott Gregson*

How can mere words begin to describe the ethereal wonder of the moments that proceeded? How can one describe sheer happiness in a sentence? Letters, words, adjectives, and verbs simply cannot do justice to the joy. The redemption. The fulfilled promises. The dreams come true. The undeserved grace of it all. Not just the magic or the happiness or the sweet details and romantic feelings, but the *wow - this is it*. The Lord is faithful. We are going to really be spending *forever* together.

All in one moment, it fell on me like an overwhelmingly good, blessed, amazing waterfall of pure love.

The man of my dreams led me past the *"Someday is today"* sign he'd hand-painted, past two stately chairs, and a beautiful little dark wooden antique table he'd purchased just for the occasion - draped in my great-great grandmothers handmade lace table runner. Pink, white and luscious red real rose petals were strewn all around and candlesticks graced the rocks on all sides. Candles were flickering absolutely *everywhere*. His beautiful viola was there, on a chair.

Tall champagne glasses and fresh gorgeous flowers (he chose them because "they look like the ones you showed me that you like for a wedding.") graced the table. Pretty pillows in my favorite colors, dotted the scene. It was a taste of heaven on earth.

By the hand, he led me through the rose petals, to a little rose-colored pillow at the end of the rock.

The sky- a watercolor canvas of blue, cream, gold and lovely hues of pink. The sea- moving and crashing, deep and wide, splashing up on me as emerald crystal blue waves crashed hard against the rocks. It felt like the two of us were out in the middle of the ocean.

He took me in his arms. Time stood still.

"Someday my prince will come...." played on. And then, he picked up his viola and played along.

Beautiful.

I didn't cry until that moment. It took a minute to "sink in." And then, as I stood there above the ocean looking at my man as he played for me, his eyes locked on mine, I lost it.

All those prayers. The lonely nights. The long years. Waiting. And waiting. And then waiting some more. The Lord…He remembered. Repeating in my mind over and over was dad's phrase: *"The word of the Lord is true. The word of the Lord is true."*

Bending down, he sweetly and carefully took my hand in his and said:

"I know you are the one for me. You are the one the Lord planned for me. I want to spend the rest of my life loving you. Forever.

Forever.

Forever!"

I wiped the tears from my eyes. Emotion filled his voice.

He reached to his back pocket and pulled out a maroon-colored little curved-top box.

He opened it up.

Sparkling, glimmering and shining. The most perfect, beautiful, dreamy engagement ring I've ever seen in my entire life.

Without thinking, my hand covered my mouth as I simultaneously smiled and cried tears of joy.

"I love you so much.

Will you marry me?"

A resounding and passionate, *YES!!!!* and a kiss.

He slipped the breathtaking ring on my finger.

Never in my life have I felt more alive. Aware. In the moment. Crystal clear. All there. Never have I felt more present.

We are going to be husband and wife!

Apparently, a bit of a crowd had gathered around on the cliff above. We didn't notice them at the time, but Mandy recorded a little video on her phone, and later when I watched, I was shocked at how loud all the cheering was. I saw him and heard him, alone. Just the two of us. The world stopped spinning. All I could see was his smiling face.

Dad later shared that as he and Mom stood up above, looking down and watching the engagement unfold, a crowd of people gathered, cheering us on, crying, and watching. He said a young mother stood near him, holding up her small son as he watched the whole scene, enraptured.

She whispered to him, "Son...someday, when you ask your Princess to marry you, this is exactly how you do it." He looked on, wide eyed. Dad couldn't help but snap a picture.

We sat on the chairs, the beautiful scene around us, crowned in love, and reveling in the joy of it all.

And, of course, I stared at my new ring.

Someday, my Prince did come. And someday is today.

The word of the Lord is true.

New York in the Fall

The next few weeks were a whirlwind. Wedding planning with my extraordinary mom began (I couldn't have done it without her!) Daniel and I bought a 1987 Airstream Sovereign, hoping to renovate and live in it someday when married.

One last gig on the East Coast, and Daniel took me with him. With real fall weather and the fact I could wear boots and a scarf in October and drink tea to warm my hands? I was delighted.

He took me to places he'd spent many lonely moments during those single years in Maryland: D.C. Alexandria: Harper's Ferry: West Virginia. There, we sat on the little balcony of an old stone building, looking out over a cobblestone street as the sun set over the hills. We Sipped spiced mulled wine as big maple leaves fell, chatting about our wedding, what being married would be like, about how far we'd come.

Magic.

The last day, we woke up early and drove from Maryland to New York City. I became emotional as we drove into the city and I spotted the Empire State Building, thinking of that picture hanging on my wall all those years in my room, come to life.

It was a perfectly crisp, fall day, and being a true California girl, I had never really experienced "autumn." He took me to all the major spots in New York City. We rode the subway, watched yellow taxis fly by, and walked through the tree-lined streets.

For lunch, he insisted we go to his family's very favorite pizza place in the city: John's on Bleeker.

I wondered why he requested a specific booth by the wall when we asked the maître de, "How long is the wait?"

Thirty minutes.

"It's okay, we can sit anywhere!" I assured him.

But, no. He was determined to sit at *that* table.

I wondered why.

While we waited, we visited Carrie Bradshaw's apartment, just a block down the street.

Back at John's, seated in Daniel's requested booth, I looked at the menu.

"Everything looks so good!" I smiled.

Daniel's eyes shined.

"I want to show you something," he whispered.

Picking up a butter knife, he asked me to lean over and showed me a little carving in the side of our bench.

"D A N + E R I N"

And half a heart.

What? I thought.

He told me the story. Of how he came here back when we started talking, almost a year before. And how today, he brought me here, on purpose, to show me.

To complete the heart.

My jaw, on the floor.

I felt like the most loved girl in all the world.

That evening, we dashed through the city, stopping at the 9/11 Memorial, the Irish Hunger Memorial, saw the Statue of Liberty from across the river, and experienced Times Square at night. We sipped drinks at the top of the Marriot Marquis at Times Square. We sat in its revolving rooftop restaurant, forty-eight stories over the Manhattan skyline, the best view of the city.

Was this real life?

We then hopped on the subway and even got to taste Serendipity's frozen hot chocolate. All in one day. Without sleeping or stopping, we ran back to our rental car and drove the distance to Maryland for our flight home. We missed it. Thanks to a gracious lady at the counter, we were booked on the next one. And home to LA we went. Life with him, a wild adventure. But I wouldn't trade it, for the world.

The Dress

The day came to try on wedding dresses. A much-dreamed of day. Mom found a random little discount shop in Simi Valley and when Mom, Mandy and I walked into the display of sparkling white, my breath caught in my chest.

We waded through the rows of tulle, silky, sparkly goodness, overwhelmed with all the choices. Choosing favorites that caught my eye. I knew the style I wanted. And I sort of just knew that I would know it was "the one" when I saw it. Sort of like I knew Daniel was "mine."

Sweetly, the lady working at the shop helped me into the big, poufy frocks of fabric as I tried on the first dress. How fun to twirl and swirl in such beautiful gowns! I modeled each dress for Mom and Mandy in front of the three large mirrors. Ducking out into the dress showroom again, Mom found a gown hanging on a discount rack in the back room. She brought it into my dressing room and said, "I just found this one….and I just want you to try it on, okay? I think it could be 'it.'"

And so, for dress #2, I slipped it on. Ivory white, made of the daintiest lace and styled so sweetly around the neckline. I slipped it on. It fit like a glove. Perfectly fitted around my hips and waist, the gorgeous train flowed behind like a bubbling white river. I stood, looking in the dressing room mirror alone as my heart beat. The way it fit, the way it looked on, the way I felt in it. I knew.

Mom and Mandy gasped and cried when I came out to model the gown for them. "It's perfect!"

We stood there, mesmerized and swooning. I just kept moving in it, back and forth. I didn't want to take it off. Two little girls wearing Disney Princess t-shirts crept around the corner – wide-eyed. "Wow, you're pretty...." Their mom ran after them, "We didn't want to spoil your moment but my girls just *had* to see the bride!"

It hit me, right then and there. Mom, Mandy, and I lost it. *The bride.* The bride! Instantly taken back to my little girl years of dreaming...imagining, hoping, praying. I stood there in *my dress* and wiped away tears. "This is the one."

The ladies who worked in the shop marveled, "It's so funny, that dress is an expensive designer gown that we've had hanging here for over a year. Many brides have tried it on but it never fit anyone...and it just fits you so perfectly. It's clearly made for you!"

The perfect fit, the perfect price, the perfect dress for me.

He is faithful, in the little dreams and big ones.

Later, as Dad paid for my dress, Mom talked to the shop owner. Back in 1984, she bought her wedding dress at a random bridal shop in Simi Valley, as well, but couldn't remember exactly where. Upon talking about the shop's history, the owner told us that there was, in fact, a bridal shop in the part of the building that is now the dressing room, in the 1980's. We were buying my dress from the very shop mom found hers at years ago!

We'd planned to go to other, fancier bridal shops later that week. To keep looking and have an elegant bridal shop fitting experience. But I was content with that magical, special day. More than I'd ever dreamed or hoped.

Cowboy Take Me Away

Mandy planned the most beautiful bridal shower for me in April. Set at a beautiful historic adobe ranch house property built in 1920, the theme was western, calling to memory all our "Little House on the Prairie" reading, watching and play acting, and also because of Daniel's Oklahoma roots and my "Cowboy" nickname for him. Every detail and special person there meant the world to me.

As I finished opening gifts, Mandy said, "I have one more present for you…" and in Daniel waltzed! Wearing his cowboy boots, jeans, and jean jacket, he handed me a bouquet of twenty-four lovely red roses! He then bowed to his knee, taking his viola to his chin and played the "Little House on the Prairie" TV show theme song. Just like Pa.

There wasn't a dry eye in the whole room. He played a few favorite songs and it was really one of the sweetest moments of my life.

At Long Last

A wedding at home, just what I always wanted.

My mama, she worked herself sick, to make sure my wedding day was just as perfect as I always imagined it to be. Dad and Daniel toiled on the land for months, preparing it to be just-right for the wedding. Our dear friend Casey Jones, a brilliant engineer, bought hundreds of twinkle lights and spent days and days hanging them about the reception area and making them work properly. My dream and vision: to have a wedding reception under the stars where all our people danced with joy as a canopy of lights above twinkled.

As Wedding Week began and "our people" trickled into town, the excitement built. Engaged in September, we purposefully chose my parent's mountain home as our venue and knew that weather could be cool or capricious before May. And so, we waited, longer than we liked, for the second week in May, so that we could be *assured* that the weather would cooperate.

And yet, the days before, sheets of rain pounded down. Hail fell. We could hardly believe our eyes.

It did not dampen our happiness! But, it was highly unheard of at our home to have anything but warm, spring weather that week.

Rain fell the night of our rehearsal dinner. The Morris family rented a mountain home nearby and moved into it for the week. They hosted the dinner and to have our two families meet? It was like heaven! They got along famously, our dearest friends adding to the mix happily.

We prayed and prayed. That the weather would accommodate. That the sun would shine. That rain would not wash away all our months of planning, all our twinkly lights, all the flowers planted and decorations hung. Our family and friends worked hard to make the day come together. A wedding at home. A labor of love. Not fancy. But elegant, charming, and really beautiful. Handmade with more love than you can imagine.

Exactly what I wanted.

The day before the wedding, the rain stopped. It was cold and damp and wet. But the rain stopped.

Our wedding day, finally came! Happiness welled in my soul! I could hardly take it in.

The day turned out perfectly, just the way I had always dreamed.

Our people came. Vows said. Daniel's song, "Praying For You" sung. Tears. Laughter. The story, culminating in one day.

And then, we danced.

The weather ended up to be quite chilly. But, no rain.

It was fitting, really. That at the end of the waiting journey, the Lord showed me, once again, that things may no go as I plan (perfect sunny weather) but His ways are better and higher. His plans are perfect. Funny thing: because of the chilly night, almost *every single wedding guest* danced! People who haven't done a jig in thirty years were up on the dance floor. It was packed. As the twinkle lights twinkled and the music played, every guest laughed and danced: rejoicing at it's finest.

And see? He uses all things for good. The cold weather, too. As He does.

I found that the ways our story and wedding were different than I'd planned or imagined were better, because His plans are better than mine. Who knew.

We honeymooned in Antigua and Barbuda in the Caribbean, and then settled into our new home by the sea in California. Grace upon grace.

Afterward

Tonight I sit, writing and sipping chamomile tea with honey and a squeeze of lemon, leaning up against our white tufted head board. My tan, sandy haired husband (*husband!*) is sleeping by my side on our white ruffled comforter.

We've been married just two months, yesterday. His sinewy arm drapes over my leg, reaching for me in his sleep, even. He breathes in and out, constant and steady. The ocean breeze blows in and out from our open window, constant and steady. The golden sand and sea is mere feet away. I can hear the waves lapping at the shore. My laptop lights up the room as I write.

How is this life?

Tonight, we are here. We're really here! In that dreamed-of place. Love is truly magic! We revel in the fulfillment of prayers and waiting. the end of a long journey. To see the Lord in new ways and feel His love. We've seen sunshine and some rain together. A magical wedding. A wonderful honeymoon full of long-awaited sweetness. Newlywed mornings.

It's all too good to be true, but it is.

We don't know what roads the Lord has planned for us, what bends they will take us down, the hills we will faithfully climb, the valleys we will forage while weeping, the mountain tops we will celebrate on. But we know we will be together, arm in arm.

Two stories intertwined, two separate lives mingled, two hearts matching, two lives melded into one.

The beauty of marriage – two become one. In every way and sense and form.

All the waiting, all the brokenness, all the wondering, all the disappointment.

More than worth it.

The happiest season, and we are savoring each sip.

Praise God from whom all blessings flow.

The dream really did come true.

At long last.

> *"It is a safe thing to trust Him*
> *to fulfill the desires which He creates."*
> *Amy Carmichael*

Isaiah 50:7

"Because the sovereign Lord helps me,
I will not be disgraced.
Therefore I will set my face like flint
and I know I will not be put to shame."

Acknowledgements

Thank you, my Lord Jesus, for...*everything.* You are and always will be my first love, the love of my life, my Prince, my Savior, my Father, and my Redeemer. Oh, what a privilege it is to live for You and to love You back. My biggest dream is to somehow make you smile.

Thank you to Daniel, my long-awaited husband. My darling. My eyes fill with tears when I think of how blessed I am to be your wife. You are the most pure-hearted and exquisite person I've ever met. It's my life's honor to love you, be romanced by you, and live our wild and free adventures. The best is yet to come, baby.

Thank you Mandy, my Sissy. My lifelong best friend, for always having my back, keeping my secrets, listening, asking, and just being there. You are the strongest person I know. Your sweetness and genuine spirit are as rare as a diamond. Your story is just beginning and it's *beautiful.* Our memories together are my comfort on rainy days. I can't imagine life without you. Love you.

Thank you, Mom, for being the Lorelai to my Rory. You are Proverbs 31. I want to be like you, someday. You have shown me what unconditional love is and I adore you. Thank you for being my editor. This project wouldn't be here without you. Now let's plan our road trips!

Thank you, Dad, for showing me what it looks like to have faith, take risks, and really fiercely love the Lord. You have taught me what is truly important in life and what ministry is. Remember when you took me to coffee at Barnes and Noble one afternoon when I was in college. You asked me, "What do you want to do with your life?" I rattled off random ideas. And then you suggested, "Why don't your write books?" I rolled my eyes, all sassy. "That's not marketable, Dad." And then, you just tilted your head and looked around *the bookstore* we sat in the middle of... Yeah. You were right. (As usual.) I love you.

To my Grandma Dot. Thank you for all the birthday dresses, "Little House" tapes, for supporting me in every way, and for always, always being "there."

To Gomie and Gompie (my great grandparents in heaven): thank you for showing me what faithfulness is.

Casey and Rose Jones: you are my second parents and I consider you family. Thank you for everything. You are gems.

To the Morris family: the sweetest in-laws I could ever dream of! Thank you for welcoming me into your family with open arms. You are all uniquely precious to me.

To Joel: I can't wait to meet you.

To Lisa: Thank you for always pointing me to Christ and His truth and for never making me feel left out when I was "the single one." Your prayers and encouragement meant the world.

To Amy Bichey: for following the Lord's lead to match us up! Because of your obedience, a new family is now established.

Jackie Rose and Ally: thank you for helping Daniel "pull off" the engagement.

To the Ranch: thank you for the memories. I miss you.

To the Point of Grace girls and Rebecca St. James: thank you for being my role models and showing me what it looked like to be cool and to love Jesus. You'll never know how much you impacted my story.

To Bruce Marchiano: for being a big brother all these years and showing me what it looks like to trust Jesus. The Lord's gift of your beautiful wife and family strengthened me to wait for my future husband.

To Rita Springer: for inviting us to worship Him with you all those years ago.

To all my wonderful Internet sisters and devoted blog readers: you are all as dear to me as any "real" friends, even though we have never met in person and are scattered all around the world. Thank you, a million, for sticking around through all my years of blogging, for your precious comments, and for understanding. This is my gift to you!

Thank you Jan Karon, Laura Ingalls Wilder, Lucy Maud Montgomery, and Louisa May Alcott for inspiring me to write. To Starbucks for your iced caramel macchiatos. And Santa Monica beach for your inspiring sunsets.

Connect with Erin

Read more at my website and blog:

www.itserinmorris.com

For inquiries, speaking requests, to share how this book impacted you, or to just say hi,

email me at: **itserinmorris@gmail.com**

COME JOIN MY PARTY ON SOCIAL MEDIA:

Instagram: itserinmorris
Twitter: itserinmorris
Periscope: itserinmorris
Pinterest.com/itserinmorris
Facebook.com/itserinjames
Snapchat: imerinmorris

CPSIA information can be obtained
at www.ICGtesting.com
Printed in the USA
FSOW04n0155301115
13880FS

9 780692 560389